THE NEW STATES OF
ABORTION POLITICS

THE NEW STATES OF ABORTION POLITICS

JOSHUA C. WILSON

stanford briefs
An Imprint of Stanford University Press
Stanford, California

Stanford University Press
Stanford, California

Printed in the United States of America
on acid-free, archival-quality paper

Library of Congress Cataloging-in-Publication Data
Wilson, Joshua C., author.
  The new states of abortion politics / Joshua C. Wilson.
Stanford, California : Stanford Briefs, an imprint of Stanford University
Press, 2016.
LCCN 2016014109 (print) | LCCN 2016014481 (ebook) |
ISBN 9780804792028 (pbk. : alk. paper) | ISBN 9781503600539
(electronic)
Subjects: LCSH: Abortion—Law and legislation—United States. |
  Abortion—Government policy—United States. | Abortion—Political
  aspects—United States. | Pro-life movement—United States.
LCC KF3771 .W55 2016 (print) | LCC KF3771 (ebook) |
  DDC 342.7308/4—dc 3
LC record available at http://lccn.loc.gov/2016014109

Typeset by Classic Typography in 10/13 Adobe Garamond

CONTENTS

For Elisha, Lila, and Reed,
who each contributed in their own ways

PREFACE

*The Professionalization
of Abortion Politics*

After nearly two decades of being upstaged by other political and "Culture War" issues, abortion politics have clearly returned to national prominence. As Daniel Becker, a leader with the National Personhood Alliance, which is dedicated to fighting abortion and related "pro-life" issues, recently stated in an interview, "I don't think we've seen a more critical election cycle [than 2016]. . . . Everything is coming to a head."[1] While various factors have contributed to the national resurgence of abortion and the current tension over it, two events in 2015 originating from the fringes of the conflict loom large in defining the popular understanding of contemporary abortion politics.

In July 2015 a group called the Center for Medical Progress (CMP) emerged on the national scene with the release of a series of edited amateur undercover videos claiming to show that Planned Parenthood engages in the callous and illegal sale of aborted fetal tissue. The videos, which include secretly recorded conversations and images of fetal tissue, came to dominate the discussion of abortion and led to federal congressional hearings on the matter, ongoing state and federal fights to defund Planned Parenthood, and a near government shutdown. Not surprisingly, the videos have also resulted in state and federal lawsuits regarding the legality of the undercover recordings and allegations that CMP engaged in racketeering, fraud, invasion of privacy, and trespassing.

In November 2015 a lone gunman killed three people and wounded nine others in an hours-long standoff with police at a Colorado Planned Parenthood clinic. The gunman, Robert Lewis Dear, is believed to have referenced the CMP videos by saying, "No more baby parts," after being taken into police custody. Less than two months later, in response to the attack, there was talk in Colorado of introducing a state bill "to increase penalties for a person convicted of blocking access to health services that include abortions."[2]

These events resonate with the contentious forms the abortion conflict took in the 1980s and 1990s. It was during this time that media coverage of abortion politics was filled with clinic bombings, the murder of abortion providers, sizeable coordinated acts of civil disobedience, and related physical and legal fights between activists. While the rates of large-scale protesting and clinic-related violence dropped off precipitously over the course of the 1990s and into the 2000s, the events of 2015 seem to suggest that they never waned. In fact the CMP videos and the Colorado Springs clinic shooting distort reality and distract from the more significant—in terms of broader policy—fight over abortion. They distort reality because of their inherent drama, and they distract because the most important disputes affecting present and future access to abortion have been principally taking place out of public view for years.

As the clinic-front activism that publicly defined abortion politics in the 1980s and early 1990s fell into decline, a well-organized and sophisticated set of "cause lawyers" and related political actors stepped into the vacuum. In doing so they redefined abortion politics. Both sides developed their legal and political resources over time, but earlier in this conflict abortion-rights activists, through standing national organizations like Planned Parenthood, had greater access to such resources. The same was not true for their opponents. While groups like Americans United for Life had been active in national politics for years, the greater antiabortion movement's elite resources were thin and diffusely distributed across the country.[3] Antiabortion advocates who faced legal problems stemming from their activism, for example, were represented in an ad hoc fashion. Simply put, the movement did not have ready and reliable access to significant numbers of well-organized, specifically dedicated, full-time lawyers.

Steps were taken during the 1990s and into the early 2000s to consolidate many of the leading Christian lawyers into a superbly organized and potent institutional structure. The effect was not only to provide activists with better legal resources but also to change the dominant form and personnel engaged in antiabortion activism. These new well-established and well-organized activist lawyers have been able to challenge abortion, not in front of clinics but in front of judges. The antiabortion movement correspondingly moved away from a seemingly doomed frontal assault on *Roe v. Wade* (1973) and the unpopular clinic-front activism of the 1980s and 1990s and adopted an incremental strategy of fighting abortion at lower jurisdictional and administrative levels. As such the politics of abortion have largely shifted to increasingly restricting abortion access as opposed to directly ending it all at once. With few exceptions this process starts in state legislatures situated in the more socially conservative regions of the country, and it continues in courtrooms as clinics and their supporting legal organizations immediately challenge the constitutionality of these laws. The process then starts anew as the actors on each side of the conflict work within the constraints established or reaffirmed by the court rulings.

The contemporary form of abortion politics now positions antiabortion activists on the offensive, where they get to experiment with the limits of abortion policy in friendly state forums and dictate the parameters of the conflict. This requires reproductive-rights advocates to respond and play defense in the courts. The former plays a long game, hoping that one day a case will reach and survive challenge in what has predominantly been an increasingly conservative US Supreme Court, potentially changing the abortion policy landscape for the entire country. The latter reacts, fighting a war of attrition, hoping to stave off another attack aimed at making the process of obtaining an abortion more costly and difficult, forcibly closing more clinics, requiring providers to present factually dubious or otherwise contested materials to patients, or stripping the ability to perform another form of abortion. This form of abortion politics, to invoke the activist quoted earlier, "is coming to a head" with the Supreme Court's hearing of *Whole Woman's Health v. Hellerstedt* (2016).

Whole Woman's Health originated in the Texas legislature as the state moved to tighten regulations on abortion clinics and push previously established legal limits. The ultimate effect of these regulations was to force a number of the state's clinics to close. While Texas was certainly not alone or even the first state legislature to attempt this, it was arguably the first state to garner national attention for its efforts—attention overwhelmingly due to Democratic state senator Wendy Davis's 2013 filibuster of the state's first attempt to pass the regulations. Since the case is reflective of a larger form of abortion politics that extends beyond Texas, it stands—however the Supreme Court decides—to significantly reform the future of the conflict.

This book tells the story of the transition to, and the current status of, the contemporary professional, institutional, and incremental politics of abortion that *Whole Woman's Health* represents. The story is told largely through the lens of another recent and significant US Supreme Court case, *McCullen v. Coakley* (2014). *McCullen* addresses a state's ability to regulate activism outside clinics by creating no-entry buffer zones around clinic entrances and exits. It is thus a story of the current standing of laws enacted during the street-politics phase of abortion when clinics were arguably on the offensive and their legal resources outmatched those of their opponents. The lawyers involved in *McCullen* debate the finer points of free speech and have little room or reason to debate abortion's legality. While this seems far afield from the traditional center of the abortion debate, this substantive distance—coupled with other qualities supplied by the court case—provides a useful means for straddling multiple decades and surveying the various changes in abortion politics and the possible future these changes suggest.

What follows are three interrelated essays built around *McCullen v. Coakley* that provide simultaneously a broad and a detailed view of contemporary abortion politics. The first essay uses Massachusetts's turbulent history of attempts to regulate antiabortion activism in front of clinics to introduce *McCullen v. Coakley* and to expose the reader to the more contentious and visible phase of abortion politics. It goes on to explore the ascent and effect of professional elites as well as the complexity of abortion politics that exists even within a state many simply assume to be liberal and in support of abortion rights.

The second essay focuses on the importance of professional legal resources for the contemporary politics of abortion. If a movement is going to be successful in court, it needs to develop or acquire and then support premier legal talent. The New Christian Right, inclusive of the antiabortion movement, has rapidly and effectively done so as evidenced by a close examination of the lawyers and legal organizations involved in *McCullen*.

The third and final essay places *McCullen v. Coakley* within the broader contexts of both the history and the contemporary state of abortion politics in order to discuss the future of the broader conflict. This essay takes a step back to better understand why abortion is a contentious issue in the United States and how the judiciary generally, and the US Supreme Court specifically, has been the formative engine of abortion politics. The essay's discussion up through Texas House Bill 2 and the resulting case of *Whole Woman's Health v. Hellerstedt* demonstrate that while the specifics change over time, the established fundamentals of the political process will likely continue to dictate the future forms of the conflict.

When, on June 26, 2014, the Supreme Court issued a mixed decision in *McCullen* to strike down the Massachusetts law regulating activism in front of clinics, it did not suddenly and fundamentally change the state and rules of abortion politics for the country. This, however, is far from evidence that the case does not matter. Rather *McCullen* stands as a potent symbol that reminds the public of the antiabortion movement's violent past—raising the specter of its possible return in the future—while exemplifying the movement's successful move toward robust institutional politics. As the case came just one year after the passage of Texas House Bill 2, its symbolic force was magnified. Together these events provided the means for the antiabortion movement to publicly announce, display, and exercise its political maturity and power while referencing a past the mainstream movement may want to avoid. As such, the case and context create an ambiguous victory and a new environment for the antiabortion movement.

McCullen is a product of developments long underway. It marks the reengagement of the Supreme Court in abortion politics; it is central to reinvigorating the public's interest in the matter, and by extension it has helped reintroduce abortion as a leading issue in electoral politics. This momentum and the resulting political opportunities for the antiabortion movement are, however, accompanied by pronounced risks. The movement's relative success has come through the combination of a viscerally invigorating issue, the development of a range of professional institutions that competently maneuver in various political forums, and over the last two decades the ability to operate largely out of the public eye. Now that abortion and other "women's issues" are once again moving toward the center stage of national politics, the antiabortion movement's success stands to reinvigorate its opponents' efforts, potentially touching off a new wave of contentious politics.

PART I VIOLENCE, LAW, AND ABORTION POLITICS

When John Salvi was identified as the lone shooter in a string of deadly attacks on three abortion clinics, a former associate of his told the press that he seemed like "just the kind of person who was ready to snap." The *New York Times* went on to report that he was "a 'weird' loner who had piled his furniture in front of the windows to block his sea view," that he was "very, very, very religious," "obsessed with his vision of the Roman Catholic religion," and that he "might be some kind of religious fanatic." His coworkers at a Portsmouth, New Hampshire, hair salon also commented that he had become increasingly unstable around the time that his parents arrived from Florida for a holiday visit. The Friday before Christmas Salvi fought with a client, and he was sent home early. His boss planned to fire him when they next met, but Salvi never returned.[1]

One week after the incident at the hair salon, on Friday, December 30, 1994, John Salvi walked into the Brookline, Massachusetts, Planned Parenthood clinic on Beacon Street and pulled a rifle out of his bag. He shot and killed Shannon Lowney, the 25-year-old receptionist, before generally opening fire on the office. Ten minutes later and two miles further down Beacon Street, Salvi walked into the Preterm Clinic, calmly asked where

he was, and then proceeded as before—killing another receptionist, Lee Ann Nichols, and spraying the room with gunfire. Richard Sarone, a clinic security guard, moved to stop Salvi and was
wounded in an exchange of gunfire. Salvi escaped but not before
dropping a bag containing a pistol and a receipt from a gun shop.[2]

In a span of approximately 30 minutes Salvi had killed two
people, wounded another five, and disappeared. The bag that he
dropped in the altercation with the Preterm Clinic security guard,
however, led investigators to discover that Salvi had bought one
thousand hollow-tip bullets from a Massachusetts gun shop. In
turn it was learned that he had purchased a Colt .22 pistol and a
Sturm Ruger semiautomatic .22 caliber rifle—the latter he had
customized with a folding stock and pistol grip—from a second
gun shop in New Hampshire. This information ultimately
brought the police to Salvi's home around 2:00 on the morning of
December 31. Although Salvi had purportedly returned there after
attacking the two clinics, he was gone when the police arrived. By
that time he was on the road heading south through the night.

A little before noon the next day Salvi walked past a small
group of protesters at the Hillcrest Clinic in Norfolk, Virginia,
and asked a clinic security guard for directions to a Burger King.
Salvi then returned to his truck, removed his black duffel bag,
pulled out his rifle, and opened fire on the clinic. While 50 to 60
people were reportedly in the clinic lobby, no one was injured in
the attack. After shooting and shattering the glass in two of the
clinic doors, Salvi got into his truck and drove off. This time,
however, the police were quickly on the scene and gave chase.
Three blocks from the clinic, Salvi threw his rifle from his truck
and surrendered.[3]

Roughly one year and three months later, Salvi was found
guilty of two counts of first-degree murder and five counts of
armed assault with intent to kill. He received two consecutive life
sentences and was taken to a maximum security prison in Massachusetts. On November 29, 1996, less than a year into his sen-

tence, John Salvi was found dead in his cell with a garbage bag around his head. His death was pronounced a suicide.

While it was known that John Salvi had strong antiabortion views, federal investigators did not have reason to think he was involved with any popular antiabortion organizations. What's more, antiabortion groups in Massachusetts were quick to distance themselves from Salvi and his use of violence. Mary McDonnell, president of the Hampton chapter of Massachusetts Citizens for Life—an early antiabortion organization and the largest in the state—was quoted the day after the shooting saying, "Anybody who professes to honor the sanctity of life and proceeds to kill people is not worthy of being called pro-life. . . . It's the worst disservice they could possibly perform [to the movement] and I deplore it." Bob Collins, also of Massachusetts Citizens for Life, commented that dramatic events like this are picked up in the media and add to the perception that all antiabortion activists are violent extremists. When an act like this occurs, Collins stated, "We try to defend ourselves right away because the 'assault media,' like assault rifles, immediately comes after us."[4]

John Salvi's "disservice" to the movement did not end with the moral stain and bad press. Salvi's rampage also directly fueled a prolonged push to strengthen laws regulating antiabortion activism in Massachusetts. This regulatory effort was not unique to the Bay State. Legal force was being marshaled and deployed against antiabortion protestors nationwide during the 1980s and 1990s. The Massachusetts story, however, stands out since it led to reopening the constitutional debate surrounding such laws more than a decade after it was presumably settled in the United States Supreme Court.

Over the course of the 1980s and 1990s abortion clinics across the country experienced an ever-increasing amount of aggressive activism and violence. According to a 1995 *Washington Post* report following the Salvi shootings, since the early 1980s there had been "123 cases of arson and 37 bombings in 33 states, and more than

1,500 cases of stalking, assault, sabotage and burglary, according to records compiled by the Bureau of Alcohol, Tobacco and Firearms (ATF) and the clinics themselves."[5] Direct action protest tactics in front of clinics accompanied this rise in overt violence. Groups like Operation Rescue, formed in 1986, had a national scope and worked to popularize clinic blockades among other tactics as a highly visible form of antiabortion activism. Many local groups adopted these aggressive strategies while providing the means for activists to confront, interact with, or simply provide witness to people accessing clinics and other facilities that provided abortion services.

While the range of approaches was diverse and many antiabortion activists worked to distance themselves from those who committed overt acts of violence and criminality, the combination of activism and violence created a pervasive sense of danger that eroded the legitimacy of antiabortion activists. It is in this context that clinics, their supporters, and sympathetic government officials mounted a more vigorous response and antiabortion activists began to challenge the resulting regulatory means in court.

At the time of Salvi's attacks Massachusetts already had a clinic access law. The federal Freedom of Access to Clinic Entrances (FACE) Act, signed into law in May 1994, also covered the Commonwealth. Together these laws prohibited clinic blockades and harassment and they reflected one strand of the legal means employed across the country to regulate antiabortion activism. The FACE Act specifically prohibits obstruction, injuries, and intimidation in front of clinics. Violations of the FACE Act may result in fines, imprisonment, or both.

The FACE Act had been subjected to constitutional challenges, which the Department of Justice's Civil Rights Division successfully defended against.[6] At the Supreme Court level, state and local laws that prohibited protesting at clinic staff members' houses (*Frisby v. Schultz*, 1988) had also been upheld as constitutional. In the 1994 case of *Madsen v. Women's Health Center, Inc.*, the Supreme Court held that a Florida court injunction regulating antiabortion protesting overstepped its constitutional limitations in various ways, but still approved of the 36-foot no-entry buffer zone around the front of abortion clinics. In *Schenck v. Pro-Choice Network of Western New York* (1997) the Court struck down the idea of "floating" buffer zones that followed people trying to access clinic services, but it again upheld the fixed buffer zone concept—in this case there were 15-foot no-entry buffers—around clinic entrances and exits. All to say that by the mid-1990s antiabortion activism already had a significant history of being regulated through court-imposed and legislative actions that created various types of buffer zones. Given the Supreme Court cases dealing with laws and injunctions regulating antiabortion protesting, clinics, courts, and legislatures had relatively clear guidance regarding what was considered constitutionally acceptable.

Strong legal precedent, the recent memory of the Salvi murders, and Massachusetts's liberal reputation should have provided a favorable environment for the state to create additional antiabortion protest regulations. This however was not the case. What instead followed demonstrates a number of things: the antiabortion movement's power; the potential for antiabortion groups to have an effect in traditionally liberal states; a recent past in which abortion stances were not so tightly tied with political party affiliation; and the ways in which state and national abortion politics are bound together. It also clearly demonstrates how important political and legal professionals have come to be for abortion politics. The story of the rise and fall of Massachusetts's pushes to additionally regulate antiabortion activism after the Salvi shootings covers almost two decades of near constant political and legal maneuvering, fighting, and reconfiguring in the state legislature and the federal courts. As will be shown, the conflict owes its long life to the creativity, dogged persistence, and increased resources of political and legal professionals who know and use all of the means available to them by their institutions.

On December 30, 1997—the third anniversary of the Brookline clinic attacks—Rep. Paul Demakis, Sen. Susan Fargo, and Rep. Ellen Story announced their sponsorship of a new abortion protest regulation bill. Their bill proposed creating 25-foot no-protest zones in front of all entrances, exits, and driveways of the state's freestanding abortion clinics. If it were to become law, first-time offenders would be fined up to $1,000 and given prison sentences of up to six months. Repeat offenses would result in fines of $500 to $5,000 and prison sentences of up to two and a half years. In its specifics the proposed bill was an amalgamation of previously affirmed regulations.

The bill's penalties were substantial but smaller than those in the FACE Act. The behavior covered, however, was broader. Whereas the FACE Act prohibited specific aggressive behaviors—such as employing force, physically obstructing, intentionally injuring, and intimidating people seeking to access clinics—the Massachusetts bill sought to prohibit antiabortion activists from simply entering a buffer zone in front of clinics. This preemptive style of regulation is seen in various court-created injunctions, and the 25-foot buffer zone proposed here was smaller than the one the Supreme Court upheld three years earlier in *Madsen*.

Considering that the bill combined aspects of previously upheld regulations and made them more modest, it seemed its supporters stood on solid constitutional ground were the law to be challenged after passage. Of more immediate concern, though, was passing the proposed law. The bill's sponsors had worked for two years with labor unions, civil libertarians, police officials, a broad spectrum of legislators, and of course abortion clinics in order to ensure their support. While the Commonwealth's American Civil Liberties Union chapter ultimately chose not to take a formal position on the 1997 bill, the chief sponsors' listening and lobbying efforts paid off in bipartisan support. Among the bill's cosponsors were legislators who consider themselves "not pro-choice" and "anti-choice." What's more, the bill had the support of the Senate president, the Senate's minority leader, Gov. Paul Cellucci, and the Attorney General.[7] Combined with Massachusetts's progressive reputation and the long list of precedents supporting antiabortion protest regulations both within the Commonwealth and across the country, one might assume the bill would quickly pass into law. Nothing could have been further from the truth.

The stalling and legislative maneuvering began almost immediately when the legislature returned from recess in January 1998. The bill's opponents had three conditions working in their favor: the bill's late submission date, the impending election year, and most importantly the support of the antiabortion Democratic Speaker of the House, Thomas Finneran. The Speaker signaled his resistance to the bill when he reportedly "told House members he would like to steer them as clear of controversy as possible during an election year, when incumbents running for re-election will have their stances on hot-button issues come under particular scrutiny by voters."[8] Although the Senate eventually passed the bill, Finneran, citing the election year, kept it from the House's agenda.

The bill resurfaced in April 1999—six months after a radical antiabortion activist killed Dr. Bernard Slepian, an abortion provider in New York. Combined with the Salvi shootings, the 1999 bill's supporters planned to stress its public safety aspects, as opposed to abortion politics, in front of the joint Criminal Justice Committee. As Rep. Story stated at the time, "I think it [the bill] is going to have difficulty getting to the floor for debate, unless he [Speaker Finneran] can be persuaded this is a public safety bill."[9]

Antiabortion forces quickly mobilized to keep the bill from making it out of committee. Antiabortion activists filled the room when the Criminal Justice Committee met to hear public comments on the bill. Those gathered made it clear through their comments and the large stickers many of them wore that they believed the proposed bill amounted to an attack on their right to free speech. As Patricia Doherty, a spokeswoman for Massachusetts Citizens for Life, argued in her statement before the committee, "This is purely and simply an attempt to squelch the speech, assembly and prayer of abortion opponents at abortion clinics."[10] After the spirited hearing, the matter was left open until a planned vote on June 21. In the intervening two months the competing sides made their arguments through public demonstrations and editorials in the state's newspapers.

As the joint Criminal Justice Committee reconvened in late June, legislative watchers predicted a narrow victory for the bill's supporters. What ensued, though, was what one abortion-rights activist observer referred to as "a slow train wreck."[11] While legislative committee members fought over procedure, the Massachusetts Catholic Conference and other antiabortion groups were "working all the grassroots."[12] Activists on both sides of the issue held rallies, marshaled letter and phone campaigns, and won support from various state newspaper editorial boards as the bill lay dormant.

Three and a half months after the committee vote to forward the bill to the Senate, the Senate voted to ask the Massachusetts Supreme Judicial Court (SJC) to issue an advisory opinion on the bill's constitutionality—a request that federal courts are barred from responding to. Since the SJC typically takes three to four months to issue such opinions, the Senate would be spared from having to vote on the bill until sometime in the next year. True to the estimate, the SJC announced on January 26, 2000, that it believed the proposed bill was constitutional on its face. With the Massachusetts Supreme Judicial Court's advisory opinion in hand, the Senate voted to approve the bill. This left five months to convince Speaker Finneran to allow the House to consider the bill.

The Speaker suggested that he would schedule a vote on the bill if the House would concurrently consider a bill that banned "partial-birth" abortions. This possibility vanished on June 28 with the US Supreme Court ruling in *Stenberg v. Carhart* (2000) that declared a similar partial-birth ban from Nebraska unconstitutional. That same day the Supreme Court also decided *Hill v. Colorado*, a case disputing Colorado's antiabortion protest regulation bill.

The Colorado "Bubble Bill," as it was known, contested in *Hill* required protestors within one hundred feet of the entrance to a health-care facility to gain permission from their intended audience in order to approach within eight feet and pass out a leaflet, display a sign, protest, educate, or counsel. If consent was not granted but a protestor persisted, she would be in violation of the law and have committed a criminal misdemeanor punishable by fines up to $750 and six months in jail. Such a protestor would also be subject to separate civil liability. Protestors more than one hundred feet from the entrance to the clinic stood outside of the law's scope and were not required to obtain the intended audience's consent before engaging in their activity.

While the Colorado Bubble Bill was different in its details from the Massachusetts buffer zone bill—creating, for example, a two-layered permeable 100-foot buffer zone versus an exclusive 25-foot zone—the underlying principles and active concepts are quite similar. The *Hill* ruling thus provided further constitutional authority for the Massachusetts bill, though it did not necessarily provide political leverage against Speaker Finneran.

With the end of the legislative session just one month away the Massachusetts bill's supporters were increasingly concerned that it would again die while waiting to be heard by the House. The bill's supporters moved to publicly pressure the Speaker into bringing the bill to the House floor. Eighty-one members of the Massachusetts House—a simple majority of its members—wrote an open letter to the Speaker asking him to put the bill on the agenda. Speaker Finneran was unmoved.

Now with just over two weeks left in the session the bill's supporters met privately with the Speaker for two consecutive days. In a move to counter, the Massachusetts Life Action League held a joint press conference with legislative members in order to attack the bill.[13] The bill's supporters, however, continued to meet with Speaker Finneran. With just days until the end of the session the bill's supporters abandoned the version passed by the Senate and offered up a less restrictive regulation. The 25-foot no-entry buffer zone was replaced by a diluted version of Colorado's Bubble Bill. While the Colorado Bubble Bill created an eight-foot zone of protection from unwanted activism around people within one hundred feet of the entrance to a clinic, the Massachusetts bill proposed a six-foot bubble around people within eighteen feet of a clinic entrance. The maximum penalties for the Massachusetts regulation were also cut in half and exemptions were made for "employees or agents of such facility acting within the scope of their employment."[14]

Finneran opened the way for the new bill to reach the House, where it passed by a substantial margin. The Senate responded by quickly passing the new bill with just one day remaining in the legislative session. The governor, as promised, signed the bill into law and it took effect in the second week of November 2000.

Reactions to the new law were mixed. The *Boston Herald* reported that some legislators viewed the last-minute bill as "a calculated 'bait and switch'" and "only a 'shell' of what it used to be."[15] Some of the bill's chief proponents who had been working on it for more than three years, however, heralded its passage as "a real victory."[16] Antiabortion activist reactions were similarly ambivalent. Ray Neary, the president of Massachusetts Committee for Life, noted that he and his organization were still opposed to the bill as an unconstitutional restriction on their free speech rights but that they were "very happy" the revised version of the bill "allows more contact and interaction with those entering the clinic than the old bill."[17]

That said, on November 8 three antiabortion activists—Mary Ann McGuire, Ruth Schiavone, and Jean Zarella—appeared in court to enjoin the new law. The three women were all regular participants in "sidewalk counseling" at Massachusetts abortion clinics where they attempted to dissuade women from seeking abortions. Their lawyer, Thomas Harvey, who was a veteran of the ongoing legal battles to regulate antiabortion activism, represented them in the Federal District Court. With their move to litigate, these women reflected and perpetuated a national pattern of enacting clinic-front regulations and then immediately and repeatedly challenging them. While the ensuing cases bear their names, the shift from the street to the courtroom is accompanied by a very real shift in who the operative actors are for the movement.

Thomas Harvey had the biography of many of the lawyers who defended antiabortion activists in the 1980s and 1990s. He graduated from a regional law school and practiced general civil litigation law. He was not what one might picture as a crusading "cause lawyer." He was however a devout Catholic and belonged to the Christian Lawyers Guild. It was at a guild meeting that he first volunteered to defend 70 members of Operation Rescue—the antiabortion organization that became nationally known for conducting massive clinic blockades in the late 1980s and early 1990s. While maintaining his general civil litigation practice, Harvey became more active in abortion politics after his work with Operation Rescue, eventually coming to serve on the board of directors for Massachusetts Citizens for Life, Pro-Life Legal Defense Fund, and A Women's Concern Pregnancy Help Center. It was through this involvement in these various antiabortion organizations that he came to challenge the Massachusetts law.[18]

The case that would be known in Federal District Court as *McGuire v. Reilly* first challenged the law's facial constitutionality. That is, it was an attempt to stop the law as patently unconstitutional before it had a chance to go into effect. The argument was primarily along two lines. First, the activists argued that the law's mere existence caused a fear that "chilled" people and kept them from engaging in otherwise protected speech activity. Second, the activists argued that the law unfairly targeted antiabortion activists while it permitted those on the other side of the debate—clinic employees—to have unrestricted access to those approaching the clinic.

Given the US Supreme Court's very recent ruling in *Hill v. Colorado*, it would at first appear that this case was an act of desperation. Not only were the two laws similar, but the Massachusetts regulation was actually *less* restrictive. Its two zones were smaller than those upheld for Colorado, and it only pertained to abortion clinics and not all health-care facilities in the state. Not surprisingly this is exactly what the Commonwealth argued in the case. Judge Edward Harrington, however, was not convinced. Rather he was swayed by the plaintiffs' argument that the narrow tailoring of the Massachusetts law to fit only abortion clinics, and the exemptions crafted for clinic employees, combined to reveal the legislature's explicit intent to regulate antiabortion activists because of the content of their speech. Of the two problems, Judge Harrington found the latter to be fatal. He concluded his opinion by remarking:

> The issue of abortion is one of the most profound moral, religious and legal issues of our time. Not since the issue of slavery tore asunder the social fabric of the Union and led to the tragedy of the Civil War, in which the blood of brothers drenched the soil of this nation in expiation of slavery's grievous crime against nature, has an issue so galvanized the intellectual and spiritual conscience of the nation. . . . It was less than thirty years ago that abortion was branded an abominable crime by most states, and considered a moral evil by most people. Pro-life advocates who firmly believe that abortion remains a grave moral evil must be given as equal an opportunity as their opponents to express to those seeking an abortion their sincere message of respect for the sanctity of innocent human life. The First Amendment requires no less.[19]

With that Judge Harrington enjoined the law ten days after it went into effect. Beyond their surprise, abortion-rights activists were infuriated by Judge Harrington's invoking the antiabortion movement's common rhetorical devices—the parallel drawn to the nation's fight over slavery and, while indirect, the labeling of abortion as "an abominable crime" and "a grave moral evil."[20]

Thomas Reilly, the named defendant and Massachusetts Attorney General, clearly disagreed with the judge's ruling, stating in the *Boston Herald*, "No one's speech is being muzzled" and that the law was simply creating a "6-foot corridor to try to defuse potentially volatile situations."[21] Looking for the means to respond in court, Reilly asked the judge to clarify the grounds for his ruling. More specifically the Commonwealth wanted to know if the judge's legal grounds for blocking the law lay with the clinic employee exemption. If that were the case, then the law could be modified and allowed to go back into effect. Reilly then appealed to the federal First Circuit Court of Appeals to lift the injunction while the law's constitutionality was in dispute. The First Circuit complied, staying the injunction and arguing that the public safety concerns motivating the law outweighed the potential detrimental effects that the law might have on activists' speech rights. With that the Massachusetts law again took effect in late December.

One month later, on January 23, 2001, the Commonwealth formally filed a lengthy appeal in defense of the law's constitutionality. The parties met in May in front of the First Circuit Court to formally dispute the law. Two new attorneys from the Pro-Life Legal Defense Fund joined Thomas Harvey in front of the First Circuit. The first lawyer listed in the court records for the appellees was Mark Rienzi. This billing was notable given that Rienzi had just graduated from Harvard Law School in 2000 and only been admitted to the bar in 2001. Although he was a stellar student—serving as an editor of the *Harvard Law Review* and earning honors both in law school and as an undergraduate at Princeton—he had no notable legal experience at the time.

The third listed attorney on the brief was Dwight G. Duncan. Unlike Rienzi, Duncan had a lengthy resume, one steeped in abortion politics and reflective of his religious faith. Duncan held a JD from Georgetown as well as two higher degrees in canon law from Pontifical University of the Holy Cross—a university in Rome started and run by Opus Dei, a division of the Catholic

Church with the intent of "contributing in a profound way to enhancing the evangelical mission of the Church throughout the world."[22] While he began his legal career working for a District of Columbia phone company, he later became a law professor at the Southern New England School of Law—now UMass Law—specializing in religious and moral issues. He was also directly linked to Thomas Harvey via his work with both the Pro-Life Legal Defense Fund and Massachusetts Citizens for Life.

Both sides of the case largely gave their now familiar arguments to the First Circuit panel—antiabortion activists charging that their speech rights were unfairly targeted, and the Commonwealth arguing that the Massachusetts law fell within the scope of the US Supreme Court's ruling in *Hill*. The lawyers for the Commonwealth added that the exemption in the law for clinic employees was inserted to allow the safe escorting of patrons to the clinic, not for enabling clinic employees to advocate for abortion.

On August 13, the Circuit Court started by complimenting the "exemplary briefing by the parties and the various amici." A veritable army of supporters comprising 32 national and state organizations, five state governments, and one Massachusetts state senator wrote five separate amicus briefs in favor of the Massachusetts law. The listed organizations included some that one would expect (for example, the NOW Legal Defense and Education Fund as well as the American College of Obstetricians and Gynecologists) and some that initially seem unrelated (for example, the American Jewish Congress, the AIDS Project of Worcester, and the YWCA of Cambridge). Three conservative Christian organizations—Massachusetts Citizens for Life, Family Research Council, and Focus on the Family—submitted two amicus briefs in support of the law's challengers. The latter two organizations submitted their brief through the American Center for Law and Justice Northeast, a branch of Pat Robertson's conservative public interest law firm that has risen to prominence in part through litigating abortion-related cases.

The First Circuit quickly found that the buffer zone law was content-neutral. The court announced that the Massachusetts law only protected against unwanted speech. What's more, "although the act clearly affects anti-abortion protesters more than other groups, there is no principled basis for assuming that this differential treatment results from a fundamental disagreement with the content of their expression." Given this, the court declared, "the district court premised its issuance of a preliminary injunction on its mistaken view that the plaintiffs probably would succeed on their First Amendment challenge. But this conclusion is insupportable."[23] With that strong rebuke the Massachusetts law was allowed to stand.

This ruling did not mark the end of *McGuire v. Reilly*. The law's opponents had limited their attack to the law as it was written, and the court had limited its ruling in kind. They were thus faced with three options. The first would be to accept the ruling and concede to living under the Massachusetts law. The second would be to appeal their "facial challenge" of the law to the US Supreme Court. The third would be to return to the District Court and challenge the law as it is applied. That is to say, they could argue that the clinic employees did more than serve as silent escorts; rather, the escorts engaged in advocacy and were thus unfairly privileged by the law.

Considering his opposition to the law and the low probability of successfully appealing to the Supreme Court, Thomas Harvey chose to file a new "as applied" suit. The Commonwealth responded to this new case by filing a motion for summary judgment. Judge Harrington, hearing the new case, was not swayed by Massachusetts's arguments for an immediate stay and granted a six-month period of discovery to "determine whether clinic employees and agents have engaged in oral protest, education or counseling within the restricted areas."[24]

A little over halfway into the discovery period the Attorney General composed and distributed a memo regarding how to enforce the clinic activism law. In brief, the Attorney General instructed Massachusetts police officers to not allow exempted parties, such as clinic employees and their agents, to counsel or educate those within the protected buffer zone. This move proved crucial in the subsequent District Court hearing regarding the unconstitutional application of the law. When the six-month discovery period ended and the case was heard, Judge Harrington announced that "the Court can identify no basis in the plaintiffs' evidence to find that the Act, as construed by the Attorney General, is being applied unconstitutionally." With this Judge Harrington granted the Attorney General's motion for summary judgment while still noting that the motion did not eliminate the possibility of future cases if facts on the ground changed.

Believing that they had proof that the law was currently not being applied evenly, Thomas Harvey filed a motion with the District Court to alter or amend the previous judgment. The new argument contended that the court had overlooked various important points of evidence of discriminatory enforcement by the police. He contended that the police had never been positioned within buffer zones, and thus they could not hear if or when clinic members were engaging in prohibited speech. The police had also never arrested or issued warnings to clinic members regarding prohibited speech, whereas they had warned and threatened antiabortion activists. Finally Harvey argued that the police officers had instructed clinic members how to be classified as people accessing the clinic, and not as clinic employees and agents, and thus avoid the Attorney General's prohibition on their counseling others within the bubble zone. Judge Harrington, however, again found that Harvey had "fail[ed] to raise a genuine issue of material fact that law enforcement officials were not evenhandedly enforcing the Attorney General's interpretation of the Act."[25] As a result the motion to alter or amend was subsequently denied.

Again undeterred, Harvey reconnected with Mark Rienzi and Dwight Duncan and appealed to the First Circuit Court. Mark Rienzi, again the lead author on the brief, had by now begun to construct the resume of a legal star on the rise. After losing the first appellate round of *McGuire* in 2001, Rienzi began a judicial clerkship for Judge Stephen F. Williams in the prestigious DC Circuit Court. Upon completing his clerkship in 2003, Rienzi joined the Supreme Court and Appellate Practice Group at Wilmer Hale LLP, a firm widely recognized as being a legal powerhouse. He now led the three-lawyer team challenging the Massachusetts law back to the First Circuit where the group made claims of both facial and applied constitutional violations. The court, finding that nothing had changed with regard to the interpretation of the facial claim, rejected it. The court also agreed with Judge Harrington that the antiabortion activists had failed to establish any meaningful pattern of unlawful and unconstitutional favoritism. Taken collectively, the First Circuit strongly rejected the antiabortion lawyers' arguments and affirmed Judge Harrington's rulings.[26] In a last-ditch attempt, the lawyers appealed to the US Supreme Court. The Court that decided *Hill v. Colorado*, however, rejected their petition in April 2005 without issuing an opinion. With that the Supreme Court seemingly ended four and a half years of doggedly persistent challenges levied in federal court against the Massachusetts law.

While the Supreme Court's decision to not hear the case would appear to end the constitutional litigation story, the Massachusetts law's most ardent supporters were—unintentionally but no less ironically—in the process of providing the ground to resurrect the challenge. The District Court, when rejecting the activists' as-applied challenge, had noted that the decision did not preclude future legal action if there were "evidence that . . . the Act's exemption for clinic employees and agents is not being enforced in accordance with the Attorney General's interpretation" or "if the Attorney General's interpretation of the Act is changed."[27] While neither of these conditions actually changed, the law itself soon would, thus opening an unforeseen opportunity for the Commonwealth's antiabortion activists.

The push to alter the Massachusetts regulation began when Thomas Finneran, the powerful Speaker of the House and the clinic law's longtime adversary, suddenly resigned from office on September 28, 2004. By June 2005 federal prosecutors would indict the former Speaker for perjury and obstruction of justice related to charges of racially motivated House redistricting. On December 28, 2005, the tenth anniversary of the Salvi shootings and exactly three months after Thomas Finneran left office, Senators Jarrett Barrios and Susan Fargo announced their sponsorship of a new clinic buffer zone bill. Claiming that the existing law allowed protestors to get too close and therefore endanger those accessing clinics and that the consent portion of the law was too difficult to understand and enforce, the new bill renewed the push for a fixed 35-foot buffer zone around entrances and driveways. In support of the enforceability problem, Planned Parenthood officials added that "last year alone, more than 40 buffer zone violations were reported to police but none were prosecuted."[28] With Finneran no longer in the legislature, the bill's supporters were confident that the bill would soon become law. The bill, however, languished until the spring of 2007.

In May 2007 the new Attorney General, Martha Coakley, accompanied by Boston police officials, legislative supporters, and representatives from the governor's office, testified at a committee hearing in favor of the 35-foot fixed buffer zone bill. The supporters' message was clear: the existing law was the flawed product of compromise. The bill passed the committee and headed to the Senate in October. On the day it passed the Senate, Eleanor McCullen, a 71-year-old grandmother who had spent the past seven years trying to dissuade women from getting abortions at the Boston Planned Parenthood Clinic, registered her disapproval to a reporter. "I'm not here to aggravate anyone. I'm just here as a last voice for women going in for an abortion. . . . We are in America. This is our sidewalk—we paid for it with our own taxes. . . . And we are gentle people."[29]

One week later the House passed the new bill by a vote of 122–28 and forwarded it on to Governor Deval Patrick. On November 13, 2007, the governor signed the bill into law, stating, "Women in the commonwealth have a right to obtain medical care free from violence, harassment or intimidation and this new law will guard that right."[30] Under the new law first-time violators of the 35-foot fixed buffer faced a fine of up to $500 and three months of jail time. Repeat offenders could be fined $5,000 and could be sent to prison for up to two and a half years.

The relative ease with which the new stricter version of the law passed demonstrates more than the importance of well-placed institutional actors like Finneran for the antiabortion movement within Massachusetts. It also suggests the antiabortion movement's waning power within that state and across the nation. In spite of the bill's supporters' claims, national data showed that clinic-front activism had become far less aggressive over the years,[31] that events like clinic killings had prompted some activists to leave the antiabortion movements, and that organizations that had driven aggressive clinic-front activism—Operation Rescue chief among them—had become significantly weakened.[32] What this masks, however, and what the subsequent history of Massachusetts's revived attempt to regulate clinic-front activism illustrates, is that the abortion politics battleground had shifted in a meaningful way in the intervening years. As a result the move to refine a law targeting an older form of activism created an opportunity for the antiabortion movement both to again challenge the Commonwealth's regulations and to exercise the movement's rapidly developing capacity in the legal arena.

Just as the previous Attorney General had with the first buffer zone law, A. G. Coakley wrote a letter of clarification to local law enforcement concerning how to implement this new buffer zone law. The letter, sent on January 16, 2008, specified that absolutely no one be allowed to loiter in the buffer zone. It also noted that those granted exemptions to be within the buffer zone—specifically clinic employees and agents, municipal employees and agents, and people just passing through the zone in order to reach a destination outside of it—were not permitted to express their opinions about abortion while within the buffer zone.

In January 2008 five new plaintiffs sought to challenge the new law in a series of cases that would all bear the name *McCullen v. Coakley*. Of the five plaintiffs four, including Eleanor McCullen, were grandparents ranging in age from 61 to 81.[33] The youngest plaintiff by 34 years was Eric Cadin, a Harvard graduate and avid surfer who would go on to become a Catholic priest.[34] All of the plaintiffs regularly prayed, held signs, distributed literature, and tried to dissuade women from getting abortions at the Boston Planned Parenthood clinic. Their facial and as-applied complaints to the federal District Court claimed that "the Act chills and deprives Plaintiffs and third parties from engaging in expressive activities guaranteed by the First and Fourteenth Amendments to the United States Constitution."[35]

While substantively very similar to the complaint and claims in the *McGuire* cases, the *McCullen* case had a notable difference from the start. Instead of being brought by a lone local attorney, *McCullen* was filed by a five-person team brought together by the Alliance Defense Fund (ADF), now known as Alliance Defending Freedom. Unlike the Pro-Life Legal Defense Fund that Thomas Harvey was affiliated with, ADF was a well-funded, full-service legal and political organization dedicated to forwarding a conservative Christian political agenda. The legal team that ADF brought to the case comprised independent lawyers from Massachusetts and Connecticut, as well as three of its lawyers from branch offices in Arizona, Kansas, and California.

The ADF first asked District Court judge Joseph Tauro for a preliminary injunction to stop the law's enforcement as the court case proceeded. Judge Tauro denied this motion and moved ahead with bench trials on the facial and as-applied challenges to the law. The competing sides submitted their written materials to the court and met to argue the facial challenge in front of the judge on May

28. Six days later the ADF team attempted to submit a postargument brief, but Judge Tauro agreed with the objections raised by the Massachusetts Attorney General's office and denied the motion.

On August 22 the court announced that it also agreed with the Attorney General's arguments that the new fixed buffer law, like its predecessor, was constitutional on its face. "Plaintiffs have fallen far short of establishing that 'no set of circumstances exists under which the Act would be valid.' Furthermore, the Act has a 'plainly legitimate sweep.' Lastly, Plaintiffs have failed to establish that the Act is impermissibly overbroad." Because the court had heard only the facial challenge, Judge Tauro closed his opinion noting that the challenge "now proceeds to Plaintiffs' as-applied challenge. A Status Conference shall be held to establish a discovery schedule and trial date."[36] The ADF team, however, decided to forgo the as-applied challenge, instead opting to move the facial challenge to the First Circuit Court of Appeals.

Nearly one year later, on July 8, 2009, and under the pen of Judge Bruce Selya, the First Circuit affirmed the District Court opinion. Judge Selya opened the decision by placing the case within its broader social movement context.

> For more than three decades, those who advocate for a woman's right to choose and those who advocate for the right to life (based on a belief that life begins at the moment of conception) have struggled for advantage in the marketplace of ideas. A series of pitched battles, forming a part of this struggle, has been waged at free-standing abortion clinics, where protestors and anti-abortion counselors seek to dissuade prospective patients, shame clinic workers, and call attention to what they perceive as the evils of voluntary terminations of pregnancies. In this campaign Massachusetts has been a battleground state. This appeal arises out of yet another skirmish in this chronicle of discord.

Continuing in the spirit of contextualizing the case, he then recounted the first Massachusetts buffer zone law's legislative history, the *McGuire* cases, and the reasons for abandoning the 2000 act in favor of the 2007 law.[37]

It was only at this point that, in Judge Selya's words, "our odyssey" turned to the now familiar legal analysis. As with all but Judge Harrington's initial 2000 *McGuire* decision, the court found in the law's favor. "The 2007 Act represents a permissible response by the Massachusetts legislature to what it reasonably perceived as a significant threat to public safety. It is content-neutral, narrowly tailored, and leaves open ample alternative channels of communication. It is, therefore, a valid time-place-manner regulation, and constitutional on its face."[38]

Like the District Court opinion, the Circuit Court concluded with the mention that an as-applied challenge was still possible. Choosing to again forgo this option, the ADF team appealed to the US Supreme Court. On March 22, 2010, the Supreme Court rejected their writ of certiorari. With all avenues for appealing the facial challenge exhausted, the ADF team—which now included Mark Rienzi who had left Wilmer Hale to be a professor at Catholic University's Columbus School of Law—returned to Judge Tauro at the District Court. The group argued in early December for both facial and as-applied challenges to the Massachusetts law. Twenty-seven days later, Judge Tauro cited the recent string of opinions against the facial challenge, the misapplication of case law, and the lack of "any new evidence, let alone 'significant new evidence'" presented by the ADF team. With a somewhat exasperated tone he automatically denied hearing the ADF's facial challenge.

Moving to the as-applied claims, Judge Tauro denied the ADF team's desire to challenge the act as being overbroad because such an argument cannot be made without also making a valid facial challenge. Citing recent precedent, he similarly dispatched the claims that the Massachusetts law is an unconstitutional prior restraint on speech, is unconstitutionally vague, a due process violation of the protestors' interest in liberty, and/or a "free exercise hybrid." While the judge conceded that the ADF team could in fact mount as-applied claims of viewpoint discrimination and equal protection violations in light of previous cases, these claims failed to meet the requisite factual bar needed to succeed.

Amid this systematic evisceration of the ADF's arguments, Judge Tauro did leave one avenue open for litigation as provided by the Attorney General's brief. "This court agrees with Defendant that . . . 'all that remains to be tried is whether the statute as applied at the clinics specified in the complaint leaves open adequate alternative channels of communication.'" Given this, the court allowed the ADF team 60 days to submit an amended brief "to the extent that it seeks to add additional abortion clinics, plaintiffs, and defendants for its as-applied claim" that the law did not allow sufficient space for people to exercise their free speech rights at specified clinics.[39]

The ADF met this deadline and the Attorney General responded with a counter-brief. After hearing some minor challenges that adjusted the clinics under review, the District Court held a bench trial at the end of August. On February 22, 2012, almost one year to the day after the amended complaint's due date and six months after the bench trial, Judge Tauro issued the District Court's opinion regarding whether activists were still able to acceptably exercise their speech rights at abortion clinics in Boston, Worcester, and Springfield, Massachusetts.

In keeping with the need to determine what events are like on the ground at these three clinics, Judge Tauro's opinion was filled with details about each location's physical layout and regular activities as recounted by activists, clinic staff, and a Commonwealth investigator. After considering the location-specific evidence, the court determined that activists had ample means to express themselves at all three clinics. As Judge Tauro noted about the Boston clinic where all but one of the plaintiffs congregated, "even though the buffer zone exists, the plaintiffs are still successful in convincing a number of women not to have abortions. Individuals entering the clinic can read Plaintiffs' signs, and clinic patients can hear Plaintiffs' prayers. Plaintiffs successfully hand out literature to people walking toward the clinic from either direction, and Plaintiffs' requests for conversation can be heard by clinic patrons both before and after they enter the buffer zone."[40]

Undeterred, the lawyers for Eleanor McCullen and her fellow antiabortion activists again appealed to the First Circuit. Notably absent this time was ADF's formal participation in the case. The legal team was now led by Mark Rienzi who was joined by two former colleagues from Wilmer Hale, as well as Philip Moran and Michael DePrimo—the two New England attorneys who had worked with the ADF from the start.

Judge Bruce Selya again penned the decision in the case, wearily announcing at its start, "This case does not come to us as a stranger. . . . The plaintiffs again appeal. They advance a salmagundi of arguments, old and new, some of which are couched in a creative recalibration of First Amendment principles." The underlying exasperation set the tone for the whole of the opinion. Judge Selya quickly worked through the case history and the site-specific data from the lower court arriving at the analysis of the legal claims. It is here that the opinion takes the tenor of a law professor addressing an ambitious yet misguided student. In reference to Rienzi's efforts to use recent cases such as the much-discussed campaign finance case *Citizens United v. FEC* (2010) to argue against the Massachusetts buffer zone law, Judge Selya responded by saying:

> This impressionistic argument, though ingenious, elevates hope over reason. The propositions for which the plaintiffs cite those cases are no more than conventional First Amendment principles recited by the Supreme Court in the context of factual scenarios far different than the scenario at issue here. . . . The plaintiffs, however, are undaunted. They seize upon an isolated statement in *Citizens United* . . . yank this statement from its context and they neglect to mention that the Court cites *Bellotti*—a case that substantially predates *McCullen* I—for this proposition.

Given this, "The Court did not retreat from its well-settled abortion clinic/buffer zone jurisprudence" when it decided *Citi-*

zens United. Moving through the other cases Rienzi's team had put forward, Judge Selya described their legal arguments as "a Rumpelstiltskin-like effort to turn straw into gold [where] the plaintiffs dismiss these important differences. . . . The short of it is that the First Amendment principles underpinning our core holdings in *McCullen* have not been materially altered, let alone abrogated, by any subsequent Supreme Court precedent."

The playful yet annoyed tone continued in the decision's analysis of the as-applied challenges. "Notwithstanding the plaintiffs' importunings, the court below concluded that adequate alternative means of communication exist at all three sites." Finally, in reference to the claim that the District Court unfairly barred the activists from amending their original legal argument, Judge Selya labeled it "a last-ditch effort to save the day." As if exhausted by listing the appeal's flaws, the decision abruptly ends in two sentences: "We need go no further. For the reasons elucidated above, we affirm the judgment of the district court."[41]

Again unfazed by a thorough rejection of their legal arguments, Rienzi and the legal team challenging the Massachusetts law made one last appeal to the US Supreme Court five years after the second round of court challenges began. The Court discussed the petition on June 20, 2013. Four days later it responded, writing, "Petition for writ of certiorari to the United States Court of Appeals for the First Circuit granted."[42] With that the Court not only likely surprised many observers but highlighted an important aspect of the new judicial context that abortion politics are played in, and in doing so raised the very real specter that it would, to echo Judge Selya, "retreat from its well-settled abortion clinic/buffer zone jurisprudence."

The lower court decisions in both *McGuire* and *McCullen* cite *Madsen v. Women's Health Center, Inc.* (1994), *Schenck v. Pro-Choice Network of Western New York* (1997), and *Hill v. Colorado* (2000) in their affirmations of the two Massachusetts regulations. In *Madsen*, *Schenck*, and *Hill* the US Supreme Court largely upheld clinic-front regulations by a vote of six to three. The majority in *Madsen* consisted of Justices Rehnquist, Blackmun, Stevens, O'Connor, Souter, and Ginsburg. Justice Breyer, Justice Blackmun's replacement on the Court, also took his place in the majority in the remaining two cases. Justices Scalia, Kennedy, and Thomas provided the dissenting votes in each case and accompanied them with passionate dissenting opinions.

In the years since the *Hill* decision the composition of the Court has seen some very significant changes and some equally significant constants. In the latter, the three vociferous dissenters in *Madsen*, *Schenck*, and *Hill* were all on the Court when *McCullen* was first filed in lower court and were still on the bench when it reached the high court. Justices Rehnquist, O'Connor, Souter, and Stevens—all members who had established the "well-settled abortion clinic/buffer zone jurisprudence"—were not. Of these departures, Rehnquist's and O'Connor's are the most significant in the decision to challenge the Massachusetts law. Chief Justice Rehnquist was replaced by the sitting Chief Justice Roberts, and Justice Alito filled the vacancy left by Justice O'Connor.

The importance of the newly composed Court for the antiabortion movement and its vastly improved legal representation was made clear by Michael DePrimo months before the case was argued in front of the US Supreme Court.

> Before I even filed the case I believed that it would be decided by the US Supreme Court. . . . And my thought was that the Supreme Court had not ruled on an injunction, I'm sorry, on an abortion buffer case since 2000. . . . My thought was that we would be about ten years out when *McCullen* would be ripe for review, and I thought that with that ten-year interim that the Supreme Court would be very interested in the case. . . . The other thing that was significant to me was that the composition of the Court changed between 2000 and 2007. . . . My thought was, we had five votes to strike down the Massachusetts statute. . . . As a matter of fact, in my opinion, I think that it is going to be a nine-zero. . . . I don't think that there is going to be a dissent. I think that all nine justices are going to vote to strike down the Massachusetts statute.[43]

The Court released its decision in the *McCullen* case on the morning of June 27, 2014, the penultimate date of its 2013–14 session. The initial news seemed to bring the worst for clinics and their supporters. Not only had the Court struck down the Massachusetts law, but as DePrimo predicted it had done so unanimously. The news however was not as bad for clinics or as monumental for the nation's antiabortion activists as it initially seemed. The 9–0 vote to strike down the Massachusetts law came through the collection of three separate and distinct opinions. As such the vote tally masks the significant internal split concerning the network of clinic access protections, including some forms of buffer zones.

Justice Alito's concurring opinion in *McCullen* is not explicit about where he stands in relation to the greater history of clinic-front regulations, but there is no doubt about Justices Scalia, Thomas, and Kennedy. As they had in past cases, these three justices took the opportunity to call for the greater undoing of Court precedent and laws governing activism in front of clinics. But this concurrence also echoes those past opinions in that it largely reads like a dissent. The tone of disappointment and anger is clear from Justice Scalia's opening lines. "Today's opinion carries forward this Court's practice of giving abortion-rights advocates a pass when it comes to suppressing the free-speech rights of their opponents. . . . There is an entirely separate, abridged edition of the First Amendment applicable to speech against abortion. . . . This [*McCullen*] is an opinion that has Something for Everyone, and the more significant portion continues the onward march of abortion-speech-only jurisprudence."

While these attacks on what Justice Scalia sees as the abridged version of the First Amendment are familiar, he makes explicit how narrow the division within the Court is: "In the present case . . . content neutrality is far from clear (the Court is divided 5–4), and the parties vigorously dispute the point."[44] Building from this, Justice Scalia returns to the past before openly calling for future challenges to this jurisprudence and pointing the direction toward the legal argument to be made.

In concluding that the statute is content based and therefore subject to strict scrutiny, I necessarily conclude that *Hill* should be overruled. . . . One final thought regarding *Hill*: It can be argued, *and it should be argued in the next case*, that by stating that "the Act would not be content neutral if it were concerned with undesirable effects that arise from . . . '[l]isteners' reactions to speech,'" . . . and then holding the Act unconstitutional for being insufficiently tailored to safety and access concerns, the Court itself has sub silentio (and perhaps inadvertently) overruled *Hill*. The unavoidable implication of that holding is that protection against unwelcome speech cannot justify restrictions on the use of public streets and sidewalks.[45]

Given the narrow split that the concurrence points to, the need for only four justices to agree in order to put an appealed case on the Court's docket, and the Roberts Court's propensity to move incrementally in effectively overruling past precedent, this advice concerning what "should be argued in the next case" seemed to carry more weight than Scalia's past calls to undo abortion clinic activism regulations. With Justice Scalia's sudden passing in February 2016, however, the future response to this call is uncertain and Justices Scalia, Thomas, and Kennedy's view of the case remains in the minority.

The controlling majority opinion in *McCullen*, written by Chief Justice Roberts and joined by Justices Ginsburg, Breyer, Sotomayor, and Kagan, is careful about specifying why Massachusetts went too far in regulating clinic-front activism. The common theme in their analysis is that the dominant politics of abortion have changed. That is, the Court no longer sees a justification for this type of strong, specifically targeted legislative response to clinic-front activism because the typical activities in front of clinics no longer pose a significant threat to those clinics or the women attempting to access them. This idea is first seen in the Court's description of the petitioners—a segment of the opinion that underscores the importance of lawyers' strategically selecting litigants for cases that challenge policy.

Some of the individuals who stand outside Massachusetts abortion clinics are fairly described as protestors, who express their moral or religious opposition to abortion through signs and chants or, in some cases, more aggressive methods such as face-to-face confrontation. Petitioners take a different tack. They attempt to engage women approaching the clinics in what they call "sidewalk counseling," which involves offering information about alternatives to abortion and help pursuing those options. . . . McCullen and the other petitioners consider it essential to maintain a caring demeanor, a calm tone of voice, and direct eye contact during these exchanges. Such interactions, petitioners believe, are much more effective means of dissuading women from having abortions than confrontational methods.[46]

The Court further minimizes the claims of clinics and their supporters by arguing that beyond the sidewalk counselors who have brought this case, those "individuals who stand outside Massachusetts abortion clinics [that] are fairly described as protestors" are outliers, have minimal disruptive effect, and are thus easily controlled. The problem, the Court implies, is that Massachusetts has not honestly tried to regulate this minority group of more aggressive activists through existing general laws on the rare occasions that the "protestors" pose a real problem.

Respondents emphasize the history in Massachusetts of obstruction at abortion clinics and the Commonwealth's allegedly failed attempts to combat such obstruction with injunctions and individual prosecutions . . . [and that] the police found it difficult to enforce the six-foot no-approach zones given the "frenetic" activity in front of clinic entrances. . . .

Although respondents claim that Massachusetts "tried other laws already on the books," [to regulate clinic-front activism] . . . they identify not a single prosecution brought under those laws within at least the last 17 years. And while the Commonwealth "tried injunctions," . . . the last injunctions they cite date to the 1990s. . . .

Far from being "widespread," the problem appears from the record to be limited principally to the Boston clinic on Saturday mornings.

Moreover, by their own account, the police appear perfectly capable of singling out lawbreakers.[47]

With contemporary antiabortion activism framed predominantly as collections of unaggressive, concerned citizens who look to calmly impart information on the public sidewalk, and generally discrediting the claims of clinic-front chaos, the Court sees the era of organized clinic blockades and violence as having passed. The Massachusetts law that banned all but a few specifically excepted types of people from coming within 35 feet of clinic entrances and driveways was thus seen as excessive and unwarranted. In the Court's words, "the Act operates to deprive petitioners of their two primary methods of communicating with patients,"[48] and the "buffer zones burden substantially more speech than necessary."[49]

In making this argument, though, these five justices go out of their way to also note that the injunctions and other existing local, state, and federal laws that regulate clinic-front activism are still valid and are in fact recommended means for clinics to control what happens in front of their doors.

> If Massachusetts determines that broader prohibitions along the same lines are necessary, it should enact legislation similar to the federal Freedom of Access to Clinics Entrances Act of 1994. . . . If the Commonwealth is particularly concerned about harassment, it could also consider an ordinance such as the one adopted in New York City that not only prohibits obstructing access to a clinic, but also makes it a crime "to follow and harass another person within 15 feet of the premises of a reproductive health care facility." . . .
>
> In addition . . . the FACE Act, and the New York City anti-harassment ordinance are all enforceable not only through criminal prosecutions but also through public and private civil actions for injunctions and other equitable relief. . . . We have previously noted the First Amendment virtues of targeted injunctions as alternative to broad, prophylactic measures. . . . In short, injunctive relief focuses on the precise individuals and the precise conduct causing a particular

problem. The Act, by contrast, categorically excludes non-exempt individuals from the buffer zones, unnecessarily sweeping in innocent individuals and their speech.[50]

Days after the decision was announced, the *Los Angeles Times* reported that "Patients and staff at the Boston clinic say they have noticed a big difference since the buffer zone law was struck down. On Wednesday, protesters walked with impunity over the yellow line that had been painted on the sidewalk after the 2007 law was passed. . . . [and] The Boston clinic has had fewer patients than normal since the Supreme Court decision came out and more skipped appointments."[51]

Massachusetts and Planned Parenthood officials did not delay in responding to the new political reality. On July 30, 2014, just about a month after the decision was announced, Governor Deval Patrick signed a new law, Bill S.2281, entitled "An Act to Promote Public Safety and Protect Access to Reproductive Health Care Facilities," which incorporates the Court's advice and reflects aspects of the federal FACE Act. The new Massachusetts law empowers the police to disperse crowds that impede access to clinics. Those cited by officials must "immediately disperse and cease to stand or be located within at least 25 feet of an entrance or a driveway to the reproductive health care facility; and the order shall remain in place for 8 hours or until the close of business of the reproductive health facility." The cease and disperse order can only be enforced, however, if "the 25-foot boundary is clearly marked" and the pertinent elements of the law "are posted outside of the reproductive health care facility."[52] Protestors who defy the law are subject to misdemeanor charges and civil damages. As expected, Massachusetts Citizens for Life has voiced its disapproval and has raised the specter of following Justice Scalia's advice by bringing suit to further dismantle the regulations that remain in front of clinics.[53]

If Massachusetts Citizens for Life decides to challenge the new law, such a move would be well suited to the increased legal institutional means of the greater antiabortion movement and also to the incremental nature of the politics of abortion today, which in turn points to the professionalization of the antiabortion movement. While this essay has introduced these themes through the broad retelling of the conflict and process that led to *McCullen v. Coakley*, the next essay will take a step back from and dig deeper into the actors and organizations involved in the case to better understand the legal professionalization of the antiabortion movement.

PART II FROM ALLIES TO ALLIANCES IN THE ANTIABORTION MOVEMENT

Thomas Harvey first became involved in abortion politics when he attended a talk that asked lawyers to volunteer to defend arrested members of Operation Rescue. The national antiabortion group had risen to prominence in the late 1980s and became the popular face of the antiabortion movement through its use of large-scale clinic blockades, among other tactics. These blockades had at least two ends. The first was to at least temporarily shut clinics down. Second, the images of people acting on and getting arrested for their beliefs would demonstrate the importance of reversing abortion's legality and mobilize the greater public's support. An additional, unintended benefit was that the resulting arrests provided a means for more lawyers to become involved in antiabortion activism—a development that would further professionalize and fundamentally change the course of abortion politics. This essay provides a detailed portrait of the resulting product of that legal professionalization process, how it is structured to be an effective counter to the reproductive-rights network and other progressive causes, and how it contrasts with the movement's earlier organizational infrastructure.

Harvey had graduated from Suffolk University Law School in Boston—a largely regional law school—and worked first as a military and then a private practice civil litigation lawyer. In the 1980s he started to volunteer with Massachusetts Citizens for Life and the Pro-Life Legal Defense Fund. Both of these groups are significant, long-standing antiabortion organizations in Massachusetts, but they are Massachusetts-specific and have little to no formal connections with national antiabortion groups or coordinated networks. As such Massachusetts Citizens for Life, the Pro-Life Legal Defense Fund, and lawyers like Thomas Harvey represent the state and face of antiabortion organizations and elite-level activism before the late 1990s and early 2000s. Understanding them and contrasting their involvement in *McGuire* with the organizations and lawyers that undertook the bulk of *McCullen* illustrates the significant changes that have occurred in the antiabortion movement in an impressively short period.

Massachusetts Citizens for Life (MCFL) was incorporated the day after the *Roe v. Wade* decision legalized abortion nationally in 1973.[1] MCFL was thus a remarkably early entrant into the post-*Roe* world of abortion politics. The popular perception of abortion politics is that Evangelical Protestants immediately rose up in opposition to *Roe* in the form of what we now know as the Christian Right. The far more accurate timeline is that the Christian Right did not really take shape until the late 1970s and that many Protestants, considering abortion to be a "Catholic issue," were likely unfazed by *Roe*.[2] Evangelical Protestants largely remained silent on abortion for a number of years after *Roe*, while a few within the faith did the preliminary work that would eventually convince them of abortion's importance and subsequently mobilize them to action.

Massachusetts, however, with its sizeable Catholic population was primed for early opposition to the Court's decision. Catholics led the pre-*Roe* movement against the state-by-state reform of abortion laws and so these activists only had to recalibrate their efforts to the new political reality. The MCFL quickly got to work connecting with other like-minded groups around the Commonwealth, organizing demonstrations, and working with the Massachusetts legislature to limit abortion access. In 1974 MCFL won notable political victories including "one of the first parental consent laws in the country, regulations for abortion facilities, an informed consent law, reporting laws on the reasons for late abortions, and requirements that abortions after 18 weeks be done in hospitals."[3] These are remarkably early previews of the type of legislative chipping away at *Roe* that has since become so popular in conservative state legislatures across the country.

Since its start, Massachusetts Citizens for Life has continually developed as an institution, demonstrating its political and organizational savvy. In 1974 it started its own newsletter—*MCFL News*—as well as an independent legal affiliate known as the Pro-Life Legal Defense Fund (PLLDF). The newsletter allowed the organization to communicate its mission, inspire and coordinate action, and keep a larger network of people engaged in the organization and the greater antiabortion cause. The formation of the PLLDF as a separate but closely affiliated organization enabled Massachusetts's antiabortion activists to engage in elite-level politics while not sacrificing attention and resources in their grassroots activism.

Six years later in 1980 Massachusetts Citizens for Life established a charitable trust, enabling the group to collect tax-deductible donations for their education programs. That same year MCFL also set up a political action committee (PAC) in time to help Ronald Reagan win the Commonwealth in his first successful bid for the presidency. The group's PACs have since entered national politics by funding multistate ads for George W. Bush's 2000 presidential run and organizing efforts in 2010 to help Scott Brown defeat Martha Coakley—the named defendant in the *McCullen* case—to fill Ted Kennedy's Senate seat. Well established, the organization now has 27 chapters across the Commonwealth and holds at least 11 significant events each year, including marches, conferences, lobbying days, trainings, and fund-raisers. Yet Massachusetts Citizens for Life is still largely limited in its mission and reach to the Bay State.

While closely connected to MCFL, the Pro-Life Legal Defense Fund was developed as a separate organization that would similarly work on abortion and other pro-life-related topics. Unlike the Massachusetts Citizens for Life, which concentrates on grassroots activism and tactics, PLLDF's focus is on elite law-centered means for political change. Over the close to 40 years since the PLLDF's establishment, it and the MCFL have grown independently of one another. Their distinct missions require different skill sets and types of activists, and so it is not surprising that they would develop separately. In fact this separation is likely key to each organization's continued success. As many scholars have argued, grassroots organizations risk being undermined when they increasingly involve lawyers.[4] Litigation and other forms of elite politics are expensive and don't readily allow for non-elites to be engaged. As a result lawyers can divert valuable resources from and alienate the non-elite members of original grassroots organizations. Intentional or not, keeping the types of organizations separate minimizes these problems.

In spite of their being distinct organizations, the continued relationship between the MCFL and PLLDF is quite evident. Massachusetts Citizens for Life has referred cases like *McGuire*, *McCullen*, and others to the Pro-Life Legal Defense Fund. What's more, many members of the PLLDF are also members of the MCFL, just as both organizations have shared common board members over time. Philip Moran, for example, is a founding member of Massachusetts Citizens for Life, a former MCFL board chair, and a former president of both organizations. He was also the local attorney for the team challenging the Massachusetts law in *McCullen*.

The Pro-Life Legal Defense Fund's first major organizational victory came in helping to write and oversee the process of passing Massachusetts's Doyle-Flynn Amendments in 1979. Similar to the federal Hyde Amendment passed in 1976, the Doyle-Flynn Amendments ended Medicaid funding of most abortions in

Massachusetts.[5] In litigation, the PLLDF's early years saw the group unsuccessfully attempt to join a case to preserve Massachusetts's parental consent law. They had more success bringing cases against Bill Baird, an early supporter of legalizing abortion and a clinic operator, cases which Moran credits with pushing Baird to close his Boston clinic.[6]

As the contentious street politics of abortion picked up after the mobilization of Evangelical Protestants against abortion in the late 1970s and into the 1980s, the PLLDF began to take more cases defending arrested antiabortion protestors. In the approximately 40 years of its existence, Phillip Moran, the group's president from 1998 to 2011, estimates that the PLLDF has taken and written amicus briefs for between 125 and 150 cases, with some years being busier than others. Overall that estimate averages to less than four cases or briefs a year. Of these cases, roughly 60 percent are related to abortion politics and the remaining 40 percent concern end-of-life issues, opposing the removal of life support and physician-assisted suicide.[7]

As of late 2013 the PLLDF comprised 12 directors, all of whom volunteer their time to the group. Of these, 11 are the attorneys who do the PLLDF's legal work. In calculating the cost of volunteering and the organization's personnel resources, Moran estimates that 90 percent of his work time is spent on his private practice and 10 percent on work related to the PLLDF. The vast majority of the group's funding, an estimated 90 percent, comes from one annual dinner fund-raiser. The remainder of the budget comes from what Moran refers to as their November "begging letter," which is distributed to a list of supporters right before the end of the tax year.[8]

Given its limited financial and personnel resources, the PLLDF is rarely able to appeal cases; it has almost no public relations arm and its activities are intensely local. The group's limitations in relation to media and publicity are underscored by its minimal web presence. The group launched a website in 2003 that it updated roughly once a month, but activity on it dropped over the course of 2004 and the site went dormant in February 2005.[9] The PLLDF relaunched its web presence in January 2014 via a newly designed website as well as the establishment of a Facebook page. The website[10] and Facebook page offer links to events and both general audience[11] and lawyer-focused blogs[12] that are infrequently updated. The PLLDF website also links to its annual newsletter, which was reestablished in 2013.[13] The organization's constrained geographic scope is illustrated by its cases, which largely pertain to the Brookline Planned Parenthood, the Brookline Country Club, and Massachusetts General Hospital—all of which are located along an eight-mile drive in metro Boston.

What's more, the PLLDF has no formal ties to similarly interested regional pro-life or antiabortion legal groups or networks. In spite of its collaborating with the Alliance Defending Freedom on *McCullen*, the PLLDF also lacks formal connections to likeminded national advocacy conglomerates.[14] Taking the group as an example of what well-established antiabortion organizations looked like before the late 1990s and early 2000s, one can see why these organizations were not as effective as they could be. Islands of volunteer lawyers simply lack the resources and thus the scope and power that come with pooled resources and coordinated efforts. Moving forward, however, the PLLDF's role in *McCullen* and its relationship to Alliance Defending Freedom show how the situation has changed, and continues to, on the national level.

By providing a degree of organization and coordination of likeminded groups and lawyers spread across the country, Alliance Defending Freedom (ADF)—formerly Alliance Defense Fund— and other conservative Christian public interest law firms and advocacy conglomerates have fundamentally altered the abilities of antiabortion and conservative Christian advocates. In Moran's words the PLLDF is "miniscule compared to those organizations. . . . [The PLLDF and organizations like the ADF] exist in separate worlds. . . . [However] most of the people at those organizations are aware of us, at least some of us as individuals. I get emails from a number of different organizations. It's just a loose, there's no, it's nothing formal."[15] The links between the older-style local legal advocacy groups and the newer generation of nationally focused advocacy conglomerates may not be formalized or appear well coordinated, and the two types of organizations seemingly exist in "separate worlds," but the personal connections Moran refers to have created a diffuse network that holds great political potential for the antiabortion movement and the greater Christian Right if it can be effectively harnessed.

Beyond facilitating this diffuse network, the newer generation of advocacy organizations also provides a wide range of concrete financial, personnel, intellectual, and media resources to the movement that allow it to compete in all political arenas without the constraints that previously hampered it. These organizations thus typify and define the legal professionalization of the antiabortion movement and the greater Christian Right, and ADF is among the most significant in their ranks. While ADF's website notes that "more than 30 prominent Christian leaders launched Alliance Defending Freedom" in the mid-1990s, they highlight

> Five exceptional men that took a leading role in forming its legal ministry. . . . They are the late Dr. Bill Bright, founder, Campus Crusade for Christ (now Cru); the late Larry Burkett, co-founder, Crown Financial Ministries; Dr. James C. Dobson, founder and chairman emeritus, Focus on the Family, and founder, *Family Talk*; the late Dr. D. James Kennedy, former senior pastor, Coral Ridge Presbyterian Church; and the late Marlin Maddoux, former host, "Point of View" radio program.[16]

Roughly a decade after its creation ADF's leadership team was still representative of prominent Christian conservative leaders and organizations. It also impressively came to include conservative Christians who are primarily known for their successes within the world of the secular legal and political elite. For example,

Roger Brooks is a partner at the prestigious white shoe law firm of Cravath, Swaine & Moore and served as an ADF board member until mid-2014;[17] Charles W. Pickering Sr. is a retired US District and Fifth Circuit Court judge who in July 2015 was still serving on the ADF board;[18] Frank Wolf represented Virginia's Tenth District in the US House of Representatives for 34 years and as of July 2015 was serving on the ADF board.[19] This expansion beyond the immediate world of the Christian Right suggests the organization's growing success and potential influence.

In the organization's own words, these early and current leaders were mobilized by "[r]ecognizing the need for a strong, coordinated legal defense. . . . Despite outstanding efforts by many Christians, *our Founders saw a battlefield in disarray with inadequate resources to win. There were allies, but no alliances. There was limited unity of effort and limited common strategy.* There was also no organized method to recruit and train Christian attorneys in modern legal challenges, and inadequate funding allowed much territory to be lost by default."[20]

The wealth of experiential, network, and financial resources offered by ADF's founding leaders immediately endowed the organization with significant potential to overcome its stated problems pertaining to united effort, common strategies, recruitment, training, and funding. While not listed on the ADF website, earlier attempts at politically organizing conservative Christians on this scale had also been hampered by theological differences and general political naiveté.[21] Moving beyond the Christian Right, author Steven Teles notes that many of the first-generation secular conservative public interest law firms were also hampered by their geographic isolation and resulting lack of national reach as well as their focus on amicus brief participation instead of mounting their own litigation strategies, which allow for more control and future funding opportunities—problems shared by the emerging Christian legal movement.[22] For the Christian Right, these same elements combined to produce a haphazard, incomplete, and local approach to litigating its interests, as seen in the discussion of the PLLDF. Looking at the five high-lighted founders and at the group's organizational structure provides a start to understanding how ADF moved to respond to these standing problems.

First, the founders' own wealth and more importantly their assumed connections to other potential funding sources addressed ADF's initial financial concerns. While ADF does not disclose its contributors, the organization now boasts the most impressive budget among the major Christian Right advocacy conglomer-ates. If one were to take snapshots over time, ADF's budget has grown from $4.7 million in 1997 to $18 million in 2003 to just shy of $40 million in fiscal year 2012.[23] This budget can be compared to the American Center for Law and Justice's (another leading conservative Christian public interest law firm) near $16 million in fiscal year 2012.[24] As shown below, by maintaining a focused mis-sion and trumpeting its own successes, ADF has effectively helped create its opportunities to raise funds. While ADF has spread its financial sources beyond its original founders, it still depends upon some large entities. Just over a quarter of the above-listed budget for 2012, for example, came from a single source, the National Christian Foundation.[25] That said, ADF's financial resources, potential, and security clearly eclipse those of the PLLDF with its almost complete dependence on an annual din-ner fund-raiser.

Beyond addressing the lack of funding, ADF also directly rec-ognizes the existence of meaningful theological differences between Christian denominations, noting that these divides are one reason why "all allied organizations do not simply 'merge' and become one." To circumvent the potential problem of theological differences, ADF explicitly does not affiliate with any one church, sect, or denomination. Instead it "simply ask[s] that all allies agree with the historical Trinitarian statement of faith (Apostles' Creed)."[26] By adopting the Trinitarian statement of faith the organization is leaving itself open to various types of Christians. In a further display of this political pragmatism ADF makes it clear that it will also work with lawyers who share some of its policy goals even if they do not fully accept the statement of faith. Such lawyers, as discussed later, have limited access to all that ADF offers.

As for ADF's overall approach to legal change, the group's adoption of a "unique combination of strategy, training, funding, and litigation"—emphasizing the first three in its first two decades—again demonstrates their nuanced diagnosis of the Christian Right's problems in the legal field and thus how to respond to them.[27] By initially downplaying its own self-generated litigation efforts, ADF was able to establish itself and move toward its stated goals of a coordinated legal effort on a nationwide level to the extent another public interest firm would not be able to. Instead of directly competing with existing firms for clients and cases, ADF focused on facilitating the efforts of those already in the movement and attracting more lawyers to this type of casework. Its training programs, as discussed in greater detail below, brought and still bring together disparate lawyers, draw in new attorneys, and foster coordinated legal strategies. Its strategic funding of cases adds to these networking and coordination efforts while also establishing the group as a rare and needed dependable source for funding litigation. In short ADF was providing the foundation for a coordinated and effective national legal effort before it began directly litigating its own cases.

ADF has since started and significantly grown its own internal litigation capabilities—a move borne out of frustration with the inability to "corral power within the movement" to the degree it originally sought.[28] This shifting of resources to better allow for independent, self-generated litigation greatly upset some in the Christian legal movement as it increased the competition for cases and resources. Since its appropriate name change from Alliance Defense Fund to Alliance Defending Freedom in 2012, its in-house legal team has come to be the top of the ADF legal network. In July 2015 the ADF website listed 51 staff attorneys specializing in a range of domestic and international cases and policy areas.[29] These lawyers are involved in bringing suits directly on behalf of ADF, and as the *New York Times* reported, they are "often involved behind the scenes, helping state officials prepare briefs justifying marriage restrictions or, in an example uncovered by RH Reality Check, a reproductive-rights website, mobilizing states to sign friend-of-the-court briefs."[30]

The expansion of ADF's functions could also be seen as the beginning of a broader loss of institutional focus, yet this was not the case. ADF still continued to "focus exclusively on legal cases and projects impacting religious liberty, the sanctity of life, and marriage and family." In doing so ADF has avoided losing its mission focus and becoming "a public policy organization." This does not mean that it did not intend to affect policy but rather that its "[f]ounders were already involved in public policy and saw the special need for this ministry's role in the judiciary."[31]

On the other hand, ADF is not entirely dedicated to abortion-related cases. By the same token, neither is the PLLDF, which is also active in other "pro-life" issues. Using ADF's US Supreme Court litigation and amicus brief submissions from 2003 to 2014 as a rough measure—one that excludes all nonlitigation and lower court activity—abortion and abortion-related cases (for example, clinic protest regulation cases) occupy 15 percent of the group's activity. This came in third behind Supreme Court case activity related to the Establishment Clause (24%) and school speech related to religion (21%), but ahead of same-sex cases (11%). Thus while ADF is not exclusively dedicated to antiabortion, it is still quite active in the area and the overwhelming bulk of its Supreme Court activity is squarely within its self-stated mission. What's more, one can argue that by combining "sanctity of life" with "religious liberty . . . and marriage and family," ADF is able to raise its profile within the Christian Right and beyond, increasing its resources and thus enabling it to represent the interests of the antiabortion movement better than it would if it were solely focused on abortion.

With the rapid expansion of its in-house legal resources ADF now more closely resembles other Christian advocacy conglomerates. A growing full-time in-house counsel reveals how the organization has changed; ADF's legal team clearly dwarfs PLLDF's collection of volunteer attorneys in numbers, resources, and case capacity dedicated to the antiabortion movement. But solely concentrating on ADF's staff attorneys would vastly underrepresent the organization's legal power. ADF is still unique in its funding of cases and its extensive training programs. It is not only still focused on its original stated substantive areas but also still committed to influencing them via the means of "strategy, training, funding, and litigation." Thus while ADF may not be *the one* center for the conservative Christian legal movement and it does now more closely resemble a public interest law firm, it is still greatly invested in growing the extensive legal network whose seeds it planted in its early days.

In Teles's discussion of the secular conservative legal movement he notes that while secular conservatives have come a long way in developing their legal resources, they are still hampered by the absence of a comparable "B Team" network of lawyers that can handle the more mundane, day-to-day tasks involved in producing social and political change through litigation. It is relatively easy to get lawyers to volunteer for high-profile cases that might make a run for the Supreme Court; it is another matter to get them to be on the watch for and take on the smaller cases that will likely be settled out of court and never garner public attention. This imbalance means that many potentially fruitful cases— including those that might be of interest to higher courts or that provide the opportunity to learn and develop new legal strategies through trial and error—are missed, and that much of the follow-up work of enforcing major case rulings is left untouched.[32] In short without a network of lawyers composing a solid B Team, the Christian Right's legal effort would continue to be incomplete and disorganized.

ADF's membership structure outside of its in-house counsel directly addresses this issue. Attorneys can become affiliated with the Alliance Defending Freedom Attorney Network at five different levels: Volunteer, Allied Attorney, Alumni Attorney, Honor Corps, and staff legal counsel. The most basic level of affiliation is as a "Volunteer." Lawyers at this level are not asked to fully agree with ADF's statement of faith or all of its policy ends. They simply have to be "willing to work on an Alliance Defending Freedom case or project or otherwise assist our legal efforts." As the website says, "Alliance Defending Freedom recognizes that attorneys who share some of our legal objectives may respectfully differ from us in their faith beliefs" and some of their political beliefs.[33]

This relative openness, as discussed above, demonstrates ADF's political pragmatism in its desire not to exclude any lawyers that could benefit its cause. Although it invites these lawyers to participate, as volunteers they are given only a small number of benefits. Volunteers receive notices about pro bono opportunities and referrals, invitations to attend trainings, and emails heralding ADF successes. While these may not be extensive benefits, they allow for the ADF network to expand to lawyers who otherwise would have been excluded in past conservative Christian political organizing efforts. Further, the benefits work as potential vehicles to higher membership levels.

The next level of ADF affiliation is at the "Allied Attorney" level. Allied attorneys can be seen as the more promising entry-level lawyers in the ADF Attorney Network because they have the clearer potential to become increasingly involved in the organization. The first marker that distinguishes allied attorneys from volunteers is that they fully subscribe to ADF's mission and statement of faith. In fact allied attorneys must sign a statement affirming their agreement to the Trinitarian statement of faith. Allied attorneys have also "completed an extensive application [and] supplied references" to ADF. They need not have previously attended an ADF training. With this vetting and demonstration of commitment, allied attorneys are given access to discounted training session fees and a range of online resources.

In direct material support for litigation allied attorneys are given access to sample briefs, pleadings, litigation manuals, grants, and other resources from the ADF legal team. Allied attorneys are also given access to ADF Google Groups and the online job/resume posting. These are significant benefits that foster the Attorney Network and advance ADF goals. The allied attorney level of membership not only provides motivated Christian lawyers with access to ADF staff but more importantly puts them in direct contact with the greater ADF Attorney Network. It is through these online means that allied attorneys can receive and provide consultation, mentorship, and encouragement. To this end the ADF website asks allied attorneys to share their "great idea for a pro bono project for [themselves] and other Allied Attorneys to help protect and reclaim religious liberty." On the same page it says that

> one of the primary goals of the Alliance Defending Freedom team is to help you succeed, both in fulfilling any short-term target and in winning your legal battles. While the team cannot promise to find cases for you, the Alliance Defending Freedom Legal Alumni website offers a number of interesting projects for your consideration as you look for pro bono opportunities. The Google Group networking forums are also used to locate volunteers for specific projects or cases. The Alliance Defending Freedom team is always willing to consult on potential cases in our core areas and to provide resources for litigating them.[34]

These quotes make it clear that ADF intends for its Google Group to work as a hothouse for developing and executing ideas that contribute to ADF's core policy areas, including fighting abortion. The job/resume list that allied attorneys also have access to provides the additional benefit—for individuals and the greater conservative Christian legal movement—of assisting lawyers to move from volunteer participation to a career in conservative Christian litigation.

A final and crucial element of allied attorney status and its relation to the organization and development of a high-functioning legal network is that there is an implied expectation that these lawyers will soon enroll in ADF trainings. These training programs are a primary means for ADF to supply intellectual resources to the movement and to create a united and coordinated litigation strategy. As the online description of the allied attorney states, this is a member who has "satisfied the requirements for attending an Alliance Defending Freedom Legal Academy, but may not have actually attended one *yet*."[35] ADF offers different types of training for different audiences. While it runs continuing legal education classes for the general legal population, its featured program for practicing attorneys is the Alliance Defending Freedom Legal Academy.

Legal Academy sessions focus on litigation strategies pertaining to ADF's three substantive areas of interest, including the sanctity of life. They are generally one and a half to two days in length—sessions run for 12 to 15 hours—and involve both educational and networking opportunities. Unlike the general continuing legal education sessions, attorneys who wish to attend regional Legal Academy sessions must be invited by an existing member of ADF's legal network. This again shows ADF's interest in screening for like-minded and dedicated lawyers and fostering a united and common legal strategy across the country.

Allied attorneys' attendance at Legal Academy sessions provides four elements that foster the ADF's Attorney Network. The trainings obviously educate the attending lawyers in legal strategies and approaches to law that ADF has deemed useful. The attending attorneys also get to meet one another and directly interact over the course of one to two days. This face time creates and strengthens bonds between members of the network, increasing the likelihood that they will successfully collaborate in the future. Furthermore attendance moves the lawyers to the next level of the ADF Attorney Network. These lawyers become "Alumni Attorneys" and are given the added benefits of access to the attorney referral network, continuing education through webinars, and confidential updates and presentations on ADF activities.

These first three elements of Legal Academy attendance work toward creating a coordinated and more effective legal movement. The fourth and likely the most important benefit for ADF specifically and the conservative Christian legal movement generally is that Legal Academy attendance comes with specified obligations. According to the ADF website,

> The goal of Alliance Defending Freedom is to create a long-term relationship with Allied Attorneys. When applying to attend an Alliance Defending Freedom Legal Academy, attorneys are simply asked to commit to report qualifying pro bono service. Alliance Defending Freedom suggests voluntary short-term targets for the amount of this service, depending upon the attorney's circumstances. The suggested target for most attorneys is 450 hours within the three years following Alliance Defending Freedom Legal Academy attendance. Attorneys who work in a large firm environment that inhibits a 450-hour commitment may opt for a three-year target of 200 hours, focused on litigation. Similarly, Alliance Defending Freedom suggests a five-year target of 150 hours for attorneys who work for the government and are prohibited from representing private clients.
>
> Alliance Defending Freedom encourages ongoing reporting of pro bono services, even if an attorney commits to a short-term target. . . .
>
> An attorney may apply to attend an Alliance Defending Freedom Legal Academy without committing to a specific short-term target of pro bono service hours; however, the willingness to make a commitment is one of several factors considered when evaluating candidates who want to attend the Alliance Defending Freedom Legal Academy.[36]

The strongly suggested commitment to provide and report pro bono services to ADF has two immediate organizational benefits.

The more obvious of the two is that this obligation provides the spur to act and to employ the means that are supplied in the form of the membership benefits described above. Using a 40-hour workweek, the suggested short-term target for the average allied attorney translates to over 11 weeks of legal services in a three-year period. Put another way that is close to one month of full-time service per year, far in excess of the American Bar Association's suggested 50-hour minimum of annual pro bono service.[37] Multiplying the 450 hours across the 2,200 allied attorneys ADF attests to have in its Attorney Network, it is clear how the ADF is harnessing the power of the diffuse Christian legal network. This number of allied attorneys contributing this many pro bono hours per year is equivalent to a law firm staffed by 165 full-time lawyers. Toward measuring ADF's production in monetary terms, the organization's website touts that it awarded its one thousandth grant in 2003—less than ten years after its founding—and in 2009 "Legal Academy-trained attorneys surpass[ed] $100 million in reported pro bono/dedicated legal service . . . since the program launched in 1997."[38]

The second benefit of this pro bono expectation comes from the reporting requirements that allow ADF to control, coordinate, and encourage its significant Attorney Network. ADF clearly acknowledges these multiple internal and external virtues of the reporting requirement in its statement to potential allied attorneys.

> A significant aspect of the Alliance Defending Freedom mission is to mobilize Christian attorneys to impact the culture by engaging the legal system. Tracking pro bono hours provides *tangible evidence of the progress* being made toward this goal. Reported pro bono service can be *used to encourage and spark mobilizing ideas* for other Allied Attorneys. And, for those who attend the Alliance Defending Freedom Legal Academy, reporting pro bono hours *demonstrates a return on investment* for the Allied Ministry Friends [donors] whose sacrificial gifts make the event possible.[39]

Reporting is also given an added competitive edge to foster the donation of service hours to the organization. "To that end, Alliance Defending Freedom recognizes significant milestones in reported pro bono service. Alliance Defending Freedom Legal Academy alumni become members of the Honor Corps upon reporting 450 hours of pro bono service. A series of Service Recognition Awards recognize members of the Honor Corps who report far more than 450 hours of service." Honor Corps membership, the highest level of nonemployee ADF affiliation, comes with the added benefits of free attendance at Legal Academy trainings and the possibility for further ADF recognition. Given that Legal Academy attendees have had to apply and be vetted to be present, one can assume a level of investment in ADF that would endow such recognition by one's peers as a significant motivator.

ADF supplies a final element of coordination, control, and discipline in its pro bono expectations by clearly specifying what counts as qualifying pro bono services. "*Pro bono* work need not involve litigation or even the representation of a client. It may involve legal research, educational presentations, or other type of work related to Alliance Defending Freedom mission areas."[40] While there is some flexibility in the form of service, there is little leeway in its substantive focus. The organization stresses that while

> Alliance Defending Freedom has allied with a number of attorneys contributing their services in efforts to dramatically increase Christian legal aid to the poor . . . *qualifying legal aid efforts should be directed in a manner that helps advance religious liberty, the sanctity of life, and marriage and family.* Some alternative programs established to aid the poor do not always support or promote biblical principles; legal aid to these programs may be reported for up to 50 hours of a 450-hour pro bono target.[41]

These qualifications for credited pro bono services help to ensure that the significant amount of legal work hours ADF inspires in its vast Attorney Network are directly targeted at the organization's core legal policy mission. This level of coordination and political specificity differentiates ADF's Attorney Network from other Christian legal pro bono organizations like the Christian Legal Society's Christian Legal Aid Program. It also supplies the final element needed to convert a diffuse network of Christian lawyers into an organized and focused legal force working together for defined policy goals.

While impressively structured, ADF is not acting alone in its efforts to organize and foster the conservative Christian legal movement. One can appreciate the extent of this rapid and strategic institutional growth by following the network of elite organizations outward from various Christian advocacy conglomerates like the Liberty Counsel and the American Center for Law and Justice (ACLJ), both of which highlight abortion as a central issue of concern.

The ACLJ is closely tied to Regent University School of Law, and Mathew Staver, the Liberty Counsel's founder, was until late 2014 the dean of Liberty University School of Law. Both of these law schools are involved in the expansion of the Christian legal network by providing future lawyers. Jerry Falwell described Liberty Law School as being founded with the "belief that we needed to produce a generation of Christian attorneys who could, in fact, infiltrate the legal profession with a strong commitment to the Judeo-Christian ethic."[42] While less overt, this idea is reflected in Regent University School of Law's statement that it provides students with "a rigorous legal education within the context of a Biblical worldview—recognizing that the legal profession is a call to much higher service."[43] In addition to this specifically Christian take on law these schools also provide opportunities for their students to engage in Christian litigation through their links to the ACLJ and the Liberty Counsel. This combination of general legal worldview and specific opportunities again feeds into supplying the conservative Christian legal movement, and by extension the antiabortion movement, with its future elite and everyday lawyers.

Alliance Defending Freedom is not directly linked to a law school but it still plays a complementary role in recruiting and training these future Christian lawyers—another means in which it supplies concrete material and intellectual resources to the movement. Interested Christian law students who may not attend the explicitly Christian law schools noted above are still able to apply to attend ADF's Blackstone Legal Fellowship. Started in 2000, this program was created to "equip Christian law students to engage the legal culture with biblical and natural law principles . . . [and] profoundly influence Christian law students to take their training and knowledge into positions of influence where they can bring about needed change in America's legal system."[44] According to its website in July 2015, "To date, over 1,500 law students from more than 200 law schools in 21 different countries have participated in Blackstone. Through Blackstone, these students have participated in internships with more than 300 different organizations and attorneys worldwide."[45]

In 2015 ADF also announced its "Young Lawyers Academy." Aimed at "recent law school graduates and lawyers in their first few years of practice, with an emphasis on those working in large and mid-size firms," the Young Lawyers Academy incorporates those who may have missed Blackstone.[46] Combined, the two programs extend avenues to the Christian legal movement beyond the handful of explicitly Christian law schools. The specific focus on lawyers from "large and mid-size firms" also suggests an interest in tapping into a more elite category of lawyer. As with the organization's other programs, this training forwards ADF's ends in a clear focus on long-term strategy.

> Whatever your area of practice, the Young Lawyers Academy will train you to effectively advocate for religious liberty, the sanctity of life, and marriage and family. . . . Not only will the Young Lawyers Academy prepare you to integrate your faith with your work, it will equip you with the tools to approach your career strategically, and connect you with an established network to provide support and guidance in a competitive and pressure-filled environment.

Your participation will also enable—and inspire—you to become part of an ever-expanding global movement to impact our legal culture. The Young Lawyers Academy connects you with outstanding like-minded Christian attorneys from around the United States, and provides an unrivaled opportunity to engage with renowned faculty and participate in a scholarly examination of issues such as natural law principles, constitutional jurisprudence, and worldview development. Daily worship and devotions will reinforce the importance of your core beliefs to your practice of law.[47]

Collectively ADF's multiple education components bring lawyers into the movement, educate them in the strategies that ADF has invested in, connect them to a broader national and international network of colleagues, and provide them the incentives and means to pursue cases coordinated to forward the group's mission. The extent and resulting power of this institutional design, which clearly reflects attention to the multiple stages of movement activity and growth, is hardly recognizable in the organizations that defined the antiabortion movement and the greater Christian Right just a few decades earlier.

Michael DePrimo, the lead attorney for the majority of *McCullen*, is an early product of this extensive Christian legal education, training, and coordinating network and an example of how these groups now work together to create a more effective professional network for the Christian Right and the antiabortion movement. DePrimo's entrance into the legal world was as a paralegal in his cousin's solo practice. When he decided that he wanted to become an attorney himself, DePrimo also knew he wanted to be trained in both state law and biblical principles. He applied to just one law school—Pat Robertson's newly created Christian Broadcasting Network University (CBNU) School of Law, soon to be renamed Regent University School of Law. He was accepted and he enrolled in 1986 in Regent's first law school class.

At the time Regent/CBNU was one of the few law schools in the country devoted to providing legal education that was explicitly linked to exploring evangelical Christian principles. But

Regent/CBNU was not the first school to provide such an education. Oral Roberts University, an evangelical Christian college
based in Tulsa, Oklahoma, welcomed its first law school class in
the fall of 1979. Oral Roberts's law school, however, closed within
less than seven years. Oral Roberts University's board of regents
then gifted its law school and law library to Christian Broadcasting
Network University School of Law. The new law school at CBNU
started classes in September 1986, received provisional accreditation from the American Bar Association in June 1989, changed its
name to Regent University School of Law in November 1989, and
secured full accreditation in August 1996.[48] While other law
schools with similar religious missions have since come into existence—Tom Monaghan's Ave Maria School of Law in 1999 and
Jerry Falwell's Liberty University School of Law in 2004—Regent
remains among the most prominent.

DePrimo received his JD from Regent in 1989 and returned to
his native Connecticut to begin a career as a real estate attorney. In
the approximately six years that he worked as a real estate lawyer
he was in terms of his practice a standard secular attorney. Beyond
his alma mater there were only two small parts of his professional
profile that hinted at an interest in pursuing Christian public
interest law. The first was his seat on the board of the Rutherford
Institute of Connecticut[49]—a state affiliate of the Rutherford
Institute, a Christian public interest law firm founded in 1982.[50]
The second was the minor bit of legal research he provided in an
abortion protestor arrest case in the early 1990s.

This all quickly changed when in 1995 the United States and
the State of Connecticut jointly accused three antiabortion activists of violating the Freedom of Access to Clinic Entrances Act.
The joint filing charged that the activists had shoved escorts,
blocked clinic access, and threatened employees at the Summit
Women's Center in Bridgeport, Connecticut. A *New York Times*
article on the filing reported that "Connecticut's Attorney General, Richard Blumenthal, said the suit was necessary to prevent

the protesters' tactics from escalating into something more violent."[51] The fear of violence was likely made all the more tangible given the geographic and temporal proximity to John Salvi's December 1994 Brookline, Massachusetts, clinic shootings that had prompted the Commonwealth to modify its clinic-front regulations.

Michael DePrimo read about the charges against the three Connecticut antiabortion activists in the newspaper and contacted his former Regent classmate Bruce Green about the case. At the time Green was the chief counsel at the American Family Association's Center for Law and Policy (CLP). Bruce Green and Benjamin Bull had collaborated as the two main architects that created the CLP in 1990. Based in Tupelo, Mississippi, the CLP was formed to represent the American Family Association (AFA) in court, litigate cases of interest to the organization, and draft model legislation that forwarded the AFA's policy agenda. Formerly known as the National Federation for Decency, the AFA was founded in 1977 and described itself as having "been on the frontlines of America's culture war" ever since.[52] According to an interview with Green in Hans Hacker's book, *The Culture of Conservative Christian Litigation*, the CLP was crafted with the intent for it to be "highly mobile, agile, and prepared. . . . [Green] stated that the CLP is capable of sending its attorneys to any part of the country in a matter of hours and appearing in court on behalf of its clients within a day. . . . 'We've tried to build a small very aggressive elite group of trial attorneys, not necessarily motion attorneys, but trial attorneys. So we've engaged in a great deal of very aggressive litigation. That's our approach.'"[53] True to this statement Green and the CLP were already aware of and working on defending the three Connecticut antiabortion activists in *US v. Vazquez*. Hearing this, Michael DePrimo volunteered his services if they were needed.

The CLP dove into *Vazquez*, renting a house to use as home base for the duration of the case.[54] According to DePrimo, there were 105 depositions conducted in the case, one of which created an opening for him to become involved in *Vazquez* and to eventually leave his real estate position for full-time Christian litigation. Green called DePrimo in the buildup to the case and asked him to represent an antiabortion activist who was being deposed and who had begun answering questions that could have criminal implications. DePrimo's performance in this role impressed Green who soon offered him a full-time position with the CLP. DePrimo took the job and moved to Tupelo within three months of stepping in on the *Vazquez* deposition.

DePrimo worked at the CLP from June 1996 until 2007, just before the organization was disbanded. While at the CLP, DePrimo was involved in drafting a regulatory ordinance for sexually oriented businesses and litigating cases where he defended street preachers and the AFA. The largest percentage of his work, however, dealt with defending antiabortion protestors. It was during this time that DePrimo was formally introduced to and became affiliated with Alliance Defending Freedom. The Center for Law and Policy was one of the organizations comprised in ADF's original network of allied firms, and DePrimo attended multiple ADF attorney trainings from the late 1990s until about 2002 when the CLP parted ways with ADF. In 2003 the CLP began a separate alliance with the Liberty Counsel and a collection of other similar firms.

The growing networks and organization of like-minded conservative Christian lawyers that ADF, the Liberty Counsel, and others were fostering, however, also contributed to the CLP's eventual demise and to tension within the movement. The Liberty Counsel, for example, which was founded at the same time as the CLP, has a history of tension with ADF that was exacerbated when ADF created its own litigation wing. In DePrimo's words, "By 2007 there were several Christian law firms that were offering pro bono services around the country. And the President and Chairman of American Family Association at the time, Don Wildmon, felt that the Center for Law and Policy at AFA had run its course. And therefore he felt that the resources that were being put towards the law center, towards the Center for Law and Policy, could be better used elsewhere."[55] Restated, it is here that one can start to see evidence of the consolidation and refinement of institutions that signify the movement's legal professionalization.

The original designers of the CLP, Bruce Green and Benjamin Bull, had left the organization far in advance of its 2007 shuttering. Both men went on to be involved in a number of today's prominent Christian legal organizations. Green left the CLP to head ADF's attorney training programs in 1998. He later left ADF to be the first dean of Jerry Falwell's Liberty University School of Law and went on to be the director of Academic Affairs and Faculty Development at the proposed Judge Paul Pressler School of Law in Louisiana—another conservative Christian law school.

Benjamin Bull similarly left the CLP to join Pat Robertson's European Center for Law and Justice (ECLJ). The ECLJ, which opened its Strasbourg, France, office in 1997, was the first international extension of Robertson's thriving domestic American Center for Law and Justice (ACLJ). Similar to ADF, the ACLJ was created in 1990 by collecting leading disparate conservative Christian lawyers, some of whom headed their own small Christian litigation firms. What's more, the newly created and well-funded ACLJ was originally housed on the Regent School of Law campus. Bull left the ECLJ in 2001 to join ADF where he is still on staff and has worked on the *McCullen* case.

DePrimo outlasted Bull and Green, staying until 2007, but he too left the CLP before its closing. Upon leaving, DePrimo did not follow the line of consolidation and join one of the emergent large Christian public interest law firms or schools. Instead he returned to Connecticut where he established a solo practice specializing in First Amendment litigation. Although he was now on his own, important parts of DePrimo's professional life remained the same. He continued with the style of work that he had performed at the

CLP, and so the majority of his cases continued to spring from the confluence of abortion politics and the First Amendment. Furthermore, although he was now a sole practitioner and had not been to an ADF training in approximately five years, his link to ADF persisted past the CLP's departure from the ADF network. DePrimo continued to scan the news for current events related to abortion politics. Just as his career with the CLP had started with his reading in the paper about a New England abortion protest case, his new career as an independent Christian legal practitioner got a significant boost from the same source.

DePrimo recalled that he and the CLP had noticed the *McGuire* case when it started, and they thought about intervening. The decision was made to pass on the case since the CLP thought that *McGuire* was both too similar and too soon after the Supreme Court's affirmation of the Colorado "Bubble Bill" in *Hill*. When in 2007 DePrimo read about Massachusetts's reforming of its buffer zone law, he felt that it was now both different and distant enough from *Hill*. The decision in *Hill* relied upon excluding uninvited speakers from approaching within a greater regulatory zone, whereas the Massachusetts law excluded all but a distinct set of speakers from a set buffer zone. A potential case would also, however, be similar enough to *Hill* to possibly affect its standing.

Beyond *Hill* DePrimo thought that a potential challenge to the Massachusetts law would be distinct from other Supreme Court cases like *Madsen* and *Schenck* that upheld broad buffer zones created through court injunctions, as opposed to laws of general application created by legislatures. The logic a favorable ruling might apply could however also have value in chipping away at these injunction cases. Considering its place in relation to these earlier cases, a possible challenge to the Massachusetts law could be decided narrowly on its own grounds or broadly, in which case it would have wider repercussions for the line of precedent regulating antiabortion direct action strategies. Finally, and possibly most important in terms of the case's future, DePrimo recognized that the Supreme Court majority which affirmed Colorado's law was no longer present—a point discussed in the previous essay.

Given all this and the entrenched forces on each side of the Massachusetts law, DePrimo felt that a case challenging the new Massachusetts law would eventually arrive at and be favorably decided by the US Supreme Court. He then reached out to Massachusetts Citizens for Life and offered his services pro bono. When MCFL accepted and put him into contact with potential plaintiffs he wrote a grant proposal for funding from ADF, putting the diffuse ADF network system into motion.

ADF quickly funded DePrimo's grant application. What's more, it also assembled a legal team to support his legal challenge. As DePrimo assessed the situation, "It was basically me versus the Attorney General's office of Massachusetts. So, obviously they have a huge staff, and I was a solo. And therefore ADF offered litigation support, some of which was having a couple of their lawyers appear on pleading. And actually appear at the hearing on the facial challenge and offer some suggestions."[56]

The original ADF team consisted of three staff attorneys from three separate ADF offices. Benjamin Bull, DePrimo's CLP predecessor, was based out of ADF's main offices in Scottsdale, Arizona, and led the first District Court team. The remaining two in-house team members' credentials reveal ADF's ability to attract new lawyers to its cause who earlier may very well have followed the more traditional tracts of elite law school graduates. Timothy Chandler from ADF's Folsom, California, office was the second attorney listed in the original District Court challenge. Chandler received his JD from UCLA—a top national law school—and became affiliated with ADF while at UCLA through ADF's Blackstone Fellowship. After graduating and joining ADF, he became involved with running the organization's Office of Strategic Training.

The third attorney, Kevin Theriot, represented ADF's Kansas office. He earned his BA from Oral Roberts University and attended Vanderbilt Law School—another leading law school—where he became involved with the Rutherford Institute in Nashville, Tennessee. Theriot worked part-time for the Rutherford Institute after graduating but soon became a staff attorney at the ACLJ. He later left the ACLJ and joined ADF in 2003 where he came to head ADF's Church Project, which is described as "a new legal effort to protect churches from excessive and unconstitutional government intrusion prohibited by the First Amendment."[57] His 2015 ADF profile adds that he is the vice president of the Center for Life.[58]

Since none of the members of the legal team were licensed to practice in Massachusetts, ADF put DePrimo in contact with Philip Moran of PLLDF. Like DePrimo, Moran had participated in ADF litigation trainings and was registered with ADF as an "allied attorney." As a result ADF was able to use its database of lawyers to locate a network attorney licensed to practice in Massachusetts, which would allow the case to go forward.

The difference between the state of the Christian legal world in 2000 when the *McGuire* case started and 2008 when *McCullen* began is stark. In 2000, organizations like ADF were still developing; a lone Christian attorney with minimal resources initially undertook a case challenging the Commonwealth of Massachusetts. When that case reached the First Circuit Court of Appeals, that lone attorney was joined by a local law professor, and the case was headed by a very recently graduated law student. Eight years later, when another lone lawyer decided to challenge the Commonwealth, he knew to contact ADF—a clear illustration of how ADF's extensive institutional investments have come to pay off with interest.

PART III THE PAST AS THE POSSIBLE FUTURE OF ABORTION POLITICS

Considering the possible future of abortion politics first requires taking a long step back before *McCullen v. Coakley* to understand how abortion policy became a constant in contemporary national politics, how and why the forms of abortion politics have changed over time, and what might reasonably influence their future course. In taking this broad view one sees that while abortion politics are complex and multiple factors influence both their form and prominence on the political stage, the judiciary generally and the United States Supreme Court specifically clearly take a leading role as the area's formative engine.

Examining the ascent and decline of various forms of abortion politics reveals the overarching importance of courts, and thus lawyers, in creating what has become the repeated pattern in abortion politics: Antiabortion activists consider their political options given their resources, the greater political climate, and a collection of other factors and then pursue a given strategy. Abortion-rights advocates respond and the antiabortion movement's tactics or its resulting gains are challenged in court. As local and appellate courts and occasionally the US Supreme Court make rulings on these challenges, they either affirm or redefine the conflict's parameters and thus the political possibilities that create the dispute's form, and the cycle starts anew. This in turn underscores the importance of lawyers, as they set the ways the courts can interact with abortion politics by first framing and then appealing cases and by making the arguments that ultimately influence judicial rulings. It is also for these reasons that looking at *McCullen* and the Court's more recent case of *Whole Woman's Health v. Hellerstedt* (2016) in light of this deeper history can help us understand what may come next.

The popular story of the beginning of contemporary abortion politics references the Court's 1973 ruling in *Roe v. Wade* as the clear starting point. There is a belief that when the Court ruled, the nation was shocked and the Christian Right immediately took to the streets, the topic instantly becoming a leading national issue. This is not what happened. At the time *Roe* was decided, conservative white evangelicals who would come to form the core of both the Christian Right and the antiabortion movement were neither organized into an active political force nor that invested in abortion as an issue. Moreover major figures within the Republican Party, which is now recognized as the political home of the Christian Right and the antiabortion movement, were actually pushing for the liberalization of abortion laws.[1] In light of this, before abortion politics took their modern form, the Christian Right needed to be created; abortion needed to be presented as a significant issue for this group; and the GOP needed to become tied to both. This process in turn had its beginning roughly one hundred years before *Roe*.

Abortion first became politicized and then criminalized over the course of the late 19th and early 20th centuries. It was at this time that the medical profession was fighting to establish itself by claiming the expertise and authority of its trained physicians and by policing this through licensing and the regulation of medical practice. This included eliminating competitors in the field such as midwives; only medical experts could truly understand, and should thus be in control of, physiological issues. The regulation of abortion became part of this process, and doctors came to control abortion with the backing of the state, which endowed them with the sole authority to choose when abortions were necessary and legal.[2]

This established the status quo that held until the 1960s and 1970s as women and some doctors began to push for the decriminalization and reform of abortion laws. The ambiguity around what qualified as a necessary (and thus legal) abortion, the tragic results of botched abortions performed on women who were uncertain of a doctor's reaction to an abortion request or who did not have the resources to consult a doctor, and concerns about fetal birth defects caused by Thalidomide and publicized by the case of Sherri Finkbine all combined to produce calls for reforming abortion law.[3] By 1973, the year that *Roe* would be decided, 17 states—many of which are today actually seeking to limit abortion access—had either liberalized or decriminalized abortion.[4] The only significant organized opposition to this multistate movement came from the Catholic Church. That ongoing political reform process was upended by the Court's decision in *Roe v. Wade* and its lesser-known companion case, *Doe v. Bolton.*

The *Roe* case challenged a Texas law that prohibited abortion except in instances where it was deemed necessary to save the life of the woman. *Doe* was a case challenging a less restrictive Georgia law that banned abortion with exceptions made for the life and health of the woman. The resulting decision striking down both laws had two important elements that would frame the future national politics of abortion.

First, the case announced that the ability to choose whether to have children, and thus the ability to access abortion, was a "fundamental right" falling under the constructed right to privacy. While not an absolute right, access to abortion as a fundamental right required a "compelling state interest" to be regulated, and any such regulations were then subject to "strict scrutiny" by the judiciary. As such the ability to access abortion was secured by the highest level of constitutional protection.

The second formative product of the decision was the creation of the sliding scale trimester system. In hearing *Roe* the Court majority cited two competing and compelling state interests. The first was in protecting the health and life of women. The second was in the "potential life" pregnant women carried. The need to balance these two interests produced the trimester system.

In brief, the Court determined that the risk of a first trimester abortion to a woman's health and life was so low, and because the fetus was not yet independently viable, that the state had little to no grounds to regulate abortion. Moving to second trimester abortions, the Court again cited the fetus's lack of viability, but it also noted the increased risk of an abortion to the woman. As a result the state did have an interest in regulating the procedure but only on behalf of the health and safety of the woman. The state could thus pass and enforce regulations that increased the procedure's safety, but it was barred from trying to dissuade from or otherwise significantly limit access to abortion.

The Court's position in relation to third trimester abortions shifted because the fetus, or the "potential life" that the woman carried, was now viable. As a result the state could now regulate abortion in order to protect that potential life. What it could not do, however, was disregard the compelling interest the woman still had in her own life and health. The state could not ban abortion outright but rather had to create exceptions to any bans in order to protect the health and life of the woman.

The specifics of this ruling created the first set of parameters and thus the range of political possibilities governing the politics of abortion for roughly the next 20 years. Restated, there were three potential avenues for those who opposed, or who would come to oppose, abortion's legality. The first and easiest was to ban abortion in the third trimester with exceptions made for preserving the health and life of the woman. The second was to regulate around abortion, including in the second trimester, to make access more difficult but in a way that was not seen as dissuading from or significantly limiting abortion access. The final option was to undo the fundamental rights status that had been given to abortion access, either through a constitutional amendment or by reversing *Roe* with another court case.

Not surprisingly the first option could be easily done in states where there was or in time would be a push to limit abortion access. The second option, indirectly regulating and limiting abortion, was pursued but it produced mixed results. The most notable national success for early abortion opponents was the Hyde Amendment, first passed in 1976, which severely limited federal funding of abortion. Other attempts to regulate abortion, such as requiring specific forms of informed, parental, and spousal consent as well as assigning waiting periods for the procedure, were largely defeated due to the application of strict scrutiny as required by *Roe*. That is, courts saw them not as narrowly tailored regulations that furthered a compelling state interest but rather as attempts by the state to illegitimately dissuade from or otherwise significantly limit access to abortion.

The final option, attacking the ruling head on through what came to be known as a "Human Life Amendment," began days after *Roe*, but these attempts overwhelmingly failed in legislative committees or at later points along the complicated constitutional amendment process. This basic pattern showed *Roe*'s resilience and led to the perpetual defeat of regulations outside of the third trimester; it continued into the late 1980s and early 1990s to the great frustration of those opposed to abortion. It is this frustration that produced the first high-profile national politics of abortion—what I have termed the street politics phase of the conflict.

This period, starting in the early 1980s and persisting into the mid-1990s, was defined by massive rallies outside of clinics and highly visible confrontations between the competing antiabortion and abortion-rights movements. Large and highly visible conflict, however, requires large and highly motivated groups of activists on both sides. Explaining how significant numbers of people came to be mobilized around abortion necessitates again returning to the 1970s and the interrelated stories of the intentional measures taken to found the Christian Right and establish abortion as a national political issue.

As noted above, the *Roe* decision did not produce an immediate or notable national backlash. Catholics who had opposed the reform movements from the 1960s and early 1970s were already mobilized and they immediately transitioned to resisting *Roe*. The Republican Party and most Protestants, however, were largely unperturbed, and many actually welcomed the decision as they had been fighting for reform.[5] Culturally conservative white evangelicals did not join Catholics in the fight to oppose abortion because at the time they were neither mobilized as a constituency nor given a reason to oppose abortion. The obvious question then is how there came to be such profound changes in both the GOP and the white evangelical community.

The shift in the Republican Party from pushing for the reform of abortion laws to the reinstatement of abortion restrictions was driven by the pursuit of advantages in electoral politics. The Republican Party first considered resisting the abortion law reform movement under President Nixon who saw a potential topic to draw conservative Catholics away from the Democratic coalition they had traditionally been a dependable part of. The pro-reform elements within the GOP were able to keep this from becoming a major issue within the party. At the same time, and in the shadow of opposition to cultural changes in the 1960s and 1970s, the contemporary social conservative wing of the party began to form.[6]

Abortion resurfaced as a divisive issue within the party in the buildup to the 1976 presidential election. Democratic candidate and Evangelical Protestant James "Jimmy" Carter announced that he was embracing a pro-*Roe* stance. This led Gerald Ford, the GOP candidate, to reluctantly adopt an anti-*Roe* stance in order to brand the Democratic Party as anti-Catholic. This was a controversial move within the GOP, which still consisted of many who supported the liberalization of abortion laws, and it did little to gain traction with Catholics, but it did encourage the growing social conservative elements within the Republican Party. The political world would shift significantly between the 1976 and 1980 presidential elections.[7]

Ronald Reagan rose as the Republican Party presidential candidate for the 1980 election. Reagan had consistently sided with the emergent socially conservative wing of the GOP in favoring an antiabortion stance. As the governor of California, with its significant white conservative evangelical community based in Southern California, he also had good reason to see the potential power to be derived from mobilizing evangelicals on the national level. The eventual role that they played in his successful election and the significance this new constituency had come to assign to abortion helped propel the GOP toward becoming solidly antiabortion. As Daniel Williams writes, when in 1976 "the Republican Party's pro-choice leadership . . . promised an antiabortion constitutional amendment . . . as a temporary political ploy . . . the platform statement instead became a rallying cry for social conservatives who used the plank to build a religiously based coalition in the GOP and drive out many of the pro-choice Republicans who had initially adopted the platform."[8] This abbreviated retelling of how the GOP came to be synonymous with the antiabortion movement only increases the need to turn to the creation of the Christian Right and abortion as a national political issue as opposed to a marginalized "Catholic issue."

As noted above, in the decades before the Reagan presidential election white Evangelical Protestants were not an organized political constituency and were distributed across the two dominant political parties. More generally though they were largely disengaged from national political life. Having once been a defining part of the American mainstream, evangelicals had been driven underground and out of the public sphere by the rise of modernity. While this was a multistage and multifaceted process, it is often summarized in the spectacle surrounding the Scopes "Monkey Trial" decided in 1925.[9]

The trial regarded the legality of teaching evolution in Tennessee's public schools, but it represented a public fight between conservative evangelical and modern scientific understandings of the world. Evangelicals won the initial legal case but lost in the court of public opinion. Feeling attacked, evangelicals retreated from public life and created their own country within a country complete with separate schools, churches, media, bookstores, and other social institutions. Collective engagement with the larger political world was discouraged and, given the creation of such a comprehensive insular community, somewhat unnecessary.

This isolation and lack of collective public organization and engagement began to change as the insular evangelical world came to feel under siege decades later. Supreme Court cases, in 1962 and 1963 respectively, barred state-sponsored school prayer and Bible reading.[10] These cases helped confirm the view within the evangelical community that they were not welcome in the public sphere. In 1978, however, the private world that they had constructed came under direct attack as the IRS threatened the tax-exempt status of Christian schools that were seen as perpetuating racial discrimination and segregation.[11] It was within this context that conservative evangelical theologians began mounting arguments for increased attention to and participation in the secular world.[12]

Part of this reentrance into the public sphere was the reframing of abortion.[13] Led by a then-obscure Swiss-based American evangelical theologian named Francis Schaeffer, abortion was presented as both a grave sin that threatened the nation's very existence and a major sign of an endemic problem—"secular humanism"—that was consuming the country. To quote the Rev. Jerry Falwell, a significant proponent of Schaeffer's message, abortion was one of many "moral cancers that are causing our society to rot from within."[14] As such, abortion in addition to "pornography, the drug epidemic, the breakdown of traditional family, [and] the establishment of homosexuality as an accepted alternative life-style" demanded immediate and profound political action by evangelicals.[15] Groups like the Moral Majority, which was established by Falwell in 1979 and is arguably the first modern Christian Right political organization, were created to provide the means for such action.

Schaeffer publicly made these arguments connecting abortion and cultural decline in his 1976 book *How Should We Then Live?* and in his 1979 book *Whatever Happened to the Human Race?* coauthored with Dr. C. Everett Koop (who would become Surgeon General under President Reagan) that specifically focused on abortion. Schaeffer also made his appeal more directly to America's Christian conservatives by going on a four-month, twenty-city US tour in 1979 with Koop to promote their book, and by converting both books into films that were, and still are, shown in churches around the country. Most significantly Schaeffer's ideas were picked up and distributed to an even greater audience by more popularly established ministers who were tapped into the evangelical cultural communication network that had been established in the preceding decades.[16] As an illustration of this power and potential, the Rev. Jerry Falwell headed a church with more than 15,000 members and his sermons were broadcast on more than three hundred stations.[17]

Galvanized by the view that they were under attack and that the country's fate lay in the balance, organized as a constituency by groups like the Moral Majority, and aimed at the Republican Party as the vehicle for realizing political change, the early Evangelical Protestant Christian Right wholly invested its energy and hopes in Ronald Reagan's 1980 presidential campaign. Reagan openly courted Christian conservatives in his now famous August 21, 1980, speech to the Religious Roundtable's National Affairs Briefing in Dallas, Texas: "Now, I know this is a non-partisan gathering and so I know that you can't endorse me, but I only brought that up because I want you to know I endorse you and what you are doing."[18] The extent of the Christian Right's infatuation with Reagan is reflected in the assembly's vocal approval of this statement. The honeymoon was relatively short.

Conservative Christians became increasingly irritated as Reagan continued to offer them lip service but failed to concretely enact their broader political agenda. Focusing on abortion specifically, the newly created Christian Right's general political naiveté led them to focus on national politics and to overinvest their hopes in the power of the presidency. What's more, the parameters *Roe* established severely limited their political options and *Roe*'s demand for strict scrutiny ended most of their seeming successes. As Williams writes, after years of the Reagan presidency "abortion was still legal, and school prayer was not."[19] Conservative Christians' frustration with the lack of change, plus the urgency that they felt in needing to reach their ends—especially in reforming the country's abortion laws—combined to create the street politics of abortion.

As noted earlier, this period of abortion politics was defined by grassroots direct action strategies staged in front of the nation's abortion clinics. Although referring to this time as the "street politics of abortion" obviously points to the importance of these clinic-front conflicts, it is not meant to deny that other important strategies were being concurrently employed. Many significant court cases and legislative actions occurred unrelated to grassroots direct action strategies. That said, the abortion conflict in the early 1980s through much of the 1990s was defined by very public confrontations between activists in front of clinics as well as by clinic violence. It was for example quite common during this time for the media to cover everything from small altercations between activists to prolonged major demonstrations and clinic bombings intended to close clinics and intimidate those who staffed them and those who sought their services. The tenor and nature of this conflict intensified as the antiabortion movement's direct action tactics became organized under national groups like Operation Rescue, founded in 1986.[20]

Strings of court-created injunctions, followed by the proliferation of local and state-level regulations similar to those seen in *McCullen v. Coakley* and capped by the federal Freedom of Access to Clinic Entrances (FACE) Act enacted in 1994, all combined to introduce the very real potential of hefty fines, bankruptcy, and imprisonment for antiabortion direct activism—especially blockades. These federal and state actions were repeatedly challenged and overwhelmingly upheld in federal appellate courts and the US Supreme Court. The Guttmacher Institute counts 15 states and the District of Columbia as possessing clinic access provisions as of June 1, 2014, and the US Supreme Court alone heard or responded to at least 14 such cases since the late 1980s.[21] Largely standing up to judicial scrutiny, these regulations helped to demobilize onetime activists and kept would-be activists from taking to the streets. This process was also complemented by other factors like the strategic placement of clinics to preclude protest space and the assassinations—both attempted and successful—of abortion providers. Collectively these elements discouraged continued street-level activism, changed the political environment, and helped raise new forms of activism that better fit the emergent political opportunities of the time.

As with the establishment of the first phases of abortion politics, the Supreme Court's rulings in these cases restructured the parameters of the conflict and antiabortion activists responded by recognizing where their new opportunities lay. In brief, as the antiabortion movement lost control of the street politics of abortion with the upholding of the regulation of clinic-front activism, the main political battlefield shifted from the visible, participatory, and volatile streets to more private, elite, and staid venues. Abortion politics since the mid-to-late 1990s became ever more concentrated on fights over limiting abortion rights and access through regulatory provisions passed at the state legislative level.[22] This has also been accompanied by new forms of direct activism that keep the grass roots of the movement alive but out of public view.

Just as the street politics of abortion did not completely end in the 1990s, the quieter state legislative strategy that defines the current phase of the conflict did not suddenly and spontaneously start at this time. As many significant political and social movements do, the wider antiabortion movement had been attempting to use any and all available means through its diffuse collective organizations. For example, Americans United for Life (AUL), which formed in 1971 as Catholics mobilized to fight the liberalization of abortion laws, had long been working to craft, pass, and subsequently help defend legislation aimed at regulating and otherwise limiting abortion access. Their approach significantly gained importance and came to define present-day abortion politics with the Supreme Court's rulings in two cases: *Webster v. Reproductive Health Services* (1989) and *Planned Parenthood of Southeastern Pennsylvania v. Casey* (1992).

Before these cases, a telling though largely unseen preview of what was to come arrived via *Thornburgh v. American College of Obstetricians & Gynecologists* (1986). This case addressed the Pennsylvania Abortion Control Act of 1982, which contained various informed consent, reporting, medical procedure, and physician requirements. The Supreme Court majority of five justices, citing "constitutional privacy interests and concerns with maternal health," struck down the law's contested provisions announcing that "States are not free, under the guise of protecting maternal health or potential life, to intimidate women into continuing pregnancies."[23]

When seen through the judicial decision alone, *Thornburgh* is solidly within the range of cases that followed *Roe*—unsuccessful attempts to employ state-level restrictive regulations struck down as violations of the standards erected earlier by the Court. *Thornburgh*'s contemporary importance, however, lies beyond the Court's decision. The potential fruits of an indirect, incremental, and long-term approach to restricting abortion access were clearly recognized and argued for in a 1985 internal Department of Justice memo on the case authored by now-sitting Supreme Court justice Samuel Alito.[24]

The memo was distributed to a limited group of seven attorneys under a cover letter from Charles Fried, special assistant to the Attorney General, stressing that Fried "need hardly say how sensitive this material is, and . . . that it have no wider circulation." In the memo, the then Justice Department attorney Alito poses the question, "What can be made of this opportunity [presented by *Thornburgh*] to advance the goals of bringing about the eventual overruling of *Roe v. Wade* and, in the meantime, of mitigating its effects?"[25] His answer in brief is that abortion opponents can use this case and related ones in the future to stress that "abortion is not unregulable,"[26] that these regulations can constitutionally be used to increase the "burden" of exercising "constitutional rights,"[27] and that such an incremental approach to attacking abortion rights is "preferable to a frontal assault on *Roe v. Wade*."[28]

Alito finishes the memo by writing, rather prophetically when considered in the larger context of the ensuing decades, that *Thornburgh*

> has most of the advantages of a brief devoted to the overruling of *Roe v. Wade*: it makes our position clear, does not tacitly concede *Roe's* legitimacy, and signals that we regard the question as live and open. At the same time, it is free of many of the disadvantages that would accompany a major effort to overturn *Roe*. When the Court hands down its decision and *Roe* is not overruled, the decision will not be portrayed as a stinging rebuke. We also will not forfeit the opportunity to address—and we will not prod the Court into summarily rejecting—the important secondary arguments outlined above.[29]

More than 30 years ago, then, Justice Alito recognized that the means of restricting abortion pursued by the State of Pennsylvania presented a promising, low-risk means of chipping away at *Roe* that was unlikely to gain much negative public attention while still having a significant functional effect on the ability to access abortion. While the Court did not side with Pennsylvania and the US Department of Justice in its *Thornburgh* decision, a change in the Court's composition started the shift that allowed for the ascent of the strategy referenced in Alito's *Thornburgh* memo.

In 1989 the Supreme Court's ruling in *Webster v. Reproductive Health Services* upheld a Missouri abortion regulation that required physicians to perform fetal viability tests on women in their 20th week or more of pregnancy and prohibited public employees and public facilities from being used in encouraging, counseling, performing, or assisting abortions that were not necessary to save the woman's life.[30] Like *Thornburgh*, *Webster* was decided in a 5–4 decision. The difference in the outcome, however, can be seen in the replacement of Justice Powell, who was in the *Thornburgh* majority, with Justice Kennedy, who was now in the *Webster* majority. Moreover AUL was involved in both the creation and legal defense of the Missouri law. This dual legislative and judicial antiabortion victory sent a clear and recognized signal about the new political opportunities for the antiabortion movement. Marshall Medoff, citing the NARAL Foundation, notes that "in the first year after the *Webster* decision, nearly 400 bills were introduced in state legislatures about abortion policy."[31]

The sign pointing antiabortion activists to state legislatures grew larger in 1992 when the Supreme Court upheld the majority of another move by Pennsylvania to limit abortion access in *Planned Parenthood of Southeastern Pennsylvania v. Casey*.[32] As in *Webster*, AUL was also involved in this case from legislation to litigation. Completing the web of connections, Justice Alito, then a judge on the Third Circuit Court of Appeals, had heard the case and employed a narrow reading of the protections afforded abortion rights in order to break from his colleagues to argue that the entire law was constitutional.

The disputed Pennsylvania law required informed consent and a 24-hour waiting period prior to receiving an abortion, parental consent for minors, and spousal notification for married women seeking abortions. The Supreme Court, like the controlling Third Circuit opinion, upheld all but the spousal notification requirement and in doing so announced,

It must be stated at the outset and with clarity that *Roe's* essential holding, the holding we reaffirm, has three parts. First is a recognition of the right of the woman to choose to have an abortion before viability and to obtain it without undue interference from the State. Before viability, the State's interests are not strong enough to support a prohibition of abortion or the imposition of a substantial obstacle to the woman's effective right to elect the procedure. Second is a confirmation of the State's power to restrict abortions after fetal viability, if the law contains exceptions for pregnancies which endanger the woman's life or health. And third is the principle that the State has legitimate interests from the outset of the pregnancy in protecting the health of the woman and the life of the fetus that may become a child.[33]

In so writing, the Court upheld a right to abortion but it also established the new lines along which antiabortion advocates could now seek to restrict abortion, and thus helped to reform the parameters and form of the greater conflict. Without wholly overruling *Roe*, *Casey* stripped away the sliding scale trimester system that more gradually balanced the rights of the woman and the emergent rights of the fetus over time. In place of the trimester system the Court imposed a two-phase understanding of the competing rights wholly riding on viability. This new way of seeing the potential nine months of pregnancy in relation to abortion moves up the point at which a state can prohibit or substantially impede abortion access. That is, the earlier one can establish viability, the earlier restrictions can come into effect. Relatedly the Court further modified the way the competing rights of the woman and the fetus are understood by establishing that the state has a legitimate interest in protecting the life of the fetus from conception, as opposed to this interest gradually increasing over the duration of the pregnancy.

Finally the Court also removed the standard of strict scrutiny that had been used to strike down earlier efforts to regulate abortion and functionally restrict access to the procedure. In place of this more restrictive standard the Court created and inserted the less defined and more subjective standard that came to be known as the "undue burden test." That is, an abortion regulation's constitutionality rode on whether or not it was seen as imposing an undue burden on the woman's ability to access an abortion.

The practical political ramifications of *Casey* are thus twofold. First, the use of fetal viability to demarcate the point at which the state's interest in regulation begins—and thus the ability to ban abortion with exceptions made for the health and life of the woman—led to an urgency to define when fetal viability occurs. That is, the earlier viability occurs according to the state, the earlier the point at which it can overwhelmingly ban abortion. For antiabortion advocates this put a premium on defending ways to move the point of viability earlier and earlier in pregnancy, or proposing alternates to viability as thresholds for when abortion can be banned.

Second, the creation of the undue burden test and the reframing of how the competing rights of the woman and the fetus are legally understood combine to open a substantial space for legislative experimentation and conflict regarding regulations in the weeks before fetal viability. While the Court insisted that "[t]hese principles do not contradict one another," the dual recognitions that women have the right to obtain an abortion before fetal viability without undue interference from the state, and that the "State has legitimate interests *from the outset of the pregnancy* in protecting the health of the woman and the life of the fetus that may become a child," can be seen at a minimum as unclear, if not in direct conflict.[34] The second post-*Casey* mission for antiabortion advocates therefore became creating legislation that limits or discourages abortion by citing the state's interests in protecting the health of women and the life of the fetus, but that would not be perceived as unduly burdensome on the previability right to abortion.

It is for these reasons that abortion debates now frequently center on regulating the space where abortions occur, on who can conduct abortions, and on claims about the health effects of receiving an abortion. These new parameters also encourage the incremental extension of the logic used to demarcate the state's versus women's interests by citing when fetuses can feel pain (a point that is not defined or agreed upon in the medical literature[35]) or when there is a detectable heartbeat as opposed to when they are viable outside of the womb.

The lowered constraints on what antiabortion activists could lobby for and defend in court, the overall perception of a friendlier US Supreme Court, the discovery of state legislatures as fruitful forums, and the prolonged increased investment in more and better professional political and legal resources (described in the previous chapter) all combined to put the antiabortion movement successfully back on the offensive. States across the country responded to the *Casey* ruling by passing more than two hundred regulations in the 13 years following the Court's decision.[36] What's more, restrictions and regulations that had previously been passed and subsequently defeated in the nation's courts were being resurrected and were now surviving challenges. The result was a redefinition of how abortion politics are defined and conducted to the present day.

The process by which new restrictions on abortion spread within these newly established political and legal parameters is well described in a *Frontline* interview with Peter Samuelson, former AUL president.

> So we're always looking for new ideas that fit within the space that *Casey* said you can regulate abortion to protect women, to exercise the state's interest in the unborn. And we're looking for those ideas. When we find those ideas, we take them out to legislators, and we take them out to allied groups that we've worked with over the last several decades. In most states we have a variety of relationships—three, four, half a dozen relationships [with] legislators and allied advocates who had been working on these issues year in, year out, and we'll start engaging in the conversation with them. . . .

Once it's passed you get a burst of publicity, and then other legislators hear about it, and they'll consider it, or it immediately gets challenged and goes into court. And then you have a pause of several years while the courts work through it. When it's ultimately upheld, which these usually are in some form or other, once it's upheld, then other legislators who have been watching that process will say: "Now we want to do that in our state. Please come help us." . . .

And so AUL is a patient group. We understand that what we need to do is create a dialogue, create situations where that dialogue can happen. And we think incrementalism is the right strategy to make that happen.

So we're very committed to that, to working in a way that through legislation—because . . . through legislation we can create conversations in states.[37]

Reflecting this, AUL and related groups have successfully used sympathetic legislatures and the frame of protecting women to directly target abortion by outlawing "partial birth" abortions and creating gestational caps on when abortions can be performed. They have also been active in promoting laws related to fetal homicide, fetal personhood, and the regulation of abortion clinic facilities that all build off this "approach of moving between legislatures and courts to further contain *Roe*."[38] As of the summer of 2015 the AUL website featured an order form for well over 40 different pieces of model legislation under the headings of "Updated Legislation in Response to Planned Parenthood Videos [related to Planned Parenthood and fetal tissue research]," "Women's Protection Project," "Abortion," "Protection of the Unborn and Newly-Born," "Rights of Conscience," and "Bioethics"—all of which include means directly and indirectly aimed at limiting abortion access and procedures.[39]

In 2010, decades into this process, state legislative activity related to abortion politics greatly accelerated. Two of the largest reasons for this come from changes in the staffing of political institutions. First, while the Supreme Court under Chief Justice Rehnquist signaled its receptivity to incrementally restricting abortion access with *Webster* and *Casey*, subsequent changes in the composition of the Court increased that signal's strength. The most important shift in this regard was the replacement of retiring justice Sandra Day O'Connor, who authored the controlling opinion in *Casey*, with the more conservative justice Samuel Alito, who forwarded the state legislative approach to abortion politics in his *Thornburgh* memo and who would have upheld the one provision that the Court struck down in *Casey*. With his addition to the Court in 2006 there appeared to be a clear majority of justices—also comprising Justices Thomas, Scalia, Kennedy, and Chief Justice Roberts—who opposed *Roe* in some capacity and who would be receptive to the continued and increased regulation of abortion.

This perception was quickly strengthened by the Court's decision under these five justices in *Gonzales v. Planned Parenthood* (2007). In brief, this case allowed the Federal Partial-Birth Abortion Ban Act to stand. This was in spite of the Court's 2000 ruling in *Stenberg v. Carhart* that struck down a similar Nebraska state law. The Court again encouraged antiabortion activists with its unanimous decision in *McCullen v. Coakley* (2014), although the case was not directly related to state restrictions on abortion access.

Coupled with the seemingly receptive Court majority, the 2010 and 2014 electoral cycles placed more state legislatures in Republican hands. After the latter election Republicans controlled "68 out of 98 partisan state legislative chambers—the highest number in the history of the party. Republicans . . . [also held] the governorship and both houses of the legislature in 23 states . . . while Democrats have that level of control in only seven."[40] Antiabortion advocates now had more potentially friendly states to lobby and reasons to be encouraged by the Court's composition; the Guttmacher Institute reported that in the timespan between 2011 and 2013 "legislatures in 30 states enacted 205 abortion restrictions—more than the total number enacted in the entire previous decade. . . . No year from 1985 through 2010 saw more than 40 new abortion restrictions; however, every year since 2011 has topped that number."[41]

As of August 1, 2015, 13 states require ultrasounds before getting an abortion, three requiring that the provider show and describe the image to the client.[42] Sixteen states have mandatory counseling requirements, including twelve requiring counseling on fetal pain, seven on the potential mental health effects of undergoing an abortion, and five on the purported link between abortion and breast cancer. Twenty-eight states have obligatory waiting periods after counseling, the majority of which are 24 hours, but Missouri, South Dakota, and Utah require 72-hour postcounseling waits—the waiting period excluding weekends and annual holidays. Finally, 38 states have parental consent and/or notification laws.[43]

Adding to this, 32 states and the District of Columbia limit state funding of abortions to those undertaken to protect the life of the woman or to end pregnancies that are the result of rape or incest. South Dakota is the sole state that will fund only abortions done to protect the life of the mother and not abortions related to rape and incest. Ten states restrict all private insurance plans and 25 states restrict insurance purchased on health exchanges from covering various abortions, though most of these restrictions still allow for abortions done to protect the life of the woman and in cases of rape or incest.[44] The overwhelming majority of states also allow for institutional or individual provider rights of refusal—42 states for the former, and 45 states for the latter.[45]

In a more novel and indirect but effective route to the goal of limiting abortion, state legislatures have passed physician, clinic, and hospital controls, which are sometimes referred to as Targeted Regulation of Abortion Providers, or TRAP laws. These laws create physical specifications for clinics as well as staffing and licensing requirements. Because they are indirect regulations, proponents often argue that they are not sought in order to limit abortion access but rather to increase women's safety and health. As of the summer of 2015, 28 states required abortion service facilities to meet physical building requirements intended for ambulatory surgical centers or hospital-admitting privilege regulations.[46] Of those with structural standards akin to those for surgical centers, 17 specify room sizes and/or corridor width and 11 require the facility to be within a certain distance from a hospital. Nineteen states also require abortion providers and/or clinics to have varying degrees of formal affiliations with local hospitals.[47] Given the costs of construction and relocation as well as the administrative and often the political difficulties associated with establishing formal affiliations with local hospitals, clinics can be devastated by these regulations.

TRAP laws as well as many of the other above-listed regulations increase the institutional and personal financial costs of abortion. They therefore add to the pressures that have decreased the number of clinics providing abortion as well as the ability of women to access them. *Time* magazine noted in its inaugural cover story for 2013 that four states possess only one surgical abortion clinic; thirteen states have less than one abortion provider per 100,000 women ages 15–44; and in that same demographic only seven states have more than five.[48]

Finally many states are combining their restrictions on access to abortion with state support for various alternatives to abortion. According again to the Guttmacher Institute, as of November 2015, 15 states offer "Choose Life" license plates in which a portion of the proceeds collected from the purchase of the plates explicitly funds "specific antichoice organizations or CPCs [crisis pregnancy centers]."[49] As of that same date nine states had either proposed or successfully enacted provisions to fund alternatives-to-abortion services.[50]

Crisis pregnancy centers, sometimes called "pregnancy resource centers," have been around for decades, but their significance within the antiabortion movement grew in tandem with the legislative politics of abortion, expanding in number and, at least within this community, prominence. CPCs typically offer information, ultrasounds, material support, and parent training with the aim of dissuading women from obtaining an abortion. Unlike abortion providers such as Planned Parenthood, they overwhelmingly do not provide health or medical services.

A 2013 *New York Times* article estimated that about 2,500 CPCs existed nationwide in comparison to approximately 1,800 abortion providers. The same article quoted Jeanneane Maxon, an administrator at Americans United for Life, as saying that CPCs "are the darlings of the pro-life movement."[51] Echoing this, CPCs have drawn public approval from such prominent political figures as President George W. Bush, former senator and Republican presidential candidate Rick Santorum, and Texas governor and Republican presidential candidate Rick Perry. More substantively and in addition to the above-listed state funding, "In 2011, Texas increased financing for the centers while cutting family planning money by two-thirds, and required abortion clinics to provide names of centers at least 24 hours before performing abortions. In South Dakota, a 2011 law being challenged by Planned Parenthood requires pregnancy center visits before abortions."[52]

Again according to Maxon, CPCs offer and thus keep alive "that ground level, one-on-one, reaching-the-woman-where-she's-at approach."[53] The people that staff these clinics are thus essentially doing the work of the old street politics' sidewalk counselors but with some important differences, which may also keep them from leaving CPCs for the streets even after the *McCullen* ruling. First, people working at CPCs are attracting the women to them instead of actively pursuing women in front of abortion clinics. Crisis pregnancy centers have done this both through the help of the state, as seen in the above examples from Texas and South Dakota, and through their own marketing strategies—some of which have been criticized as deceptive. They have also done this through their own site location, situating both mobile and fixed CPCs near or across from abortion clinics.[54]

In addition to avoiding the standing risks of violating laws regulating clinic-front activism, attracting women to CPCs allows these activists various advantages over making their claims on the street.

Unlike sidewalk counselors, CPCs can employ technology like sonograms and ultrasounds in their efforts to dissuade women from having abortions. Furthermore the controlled environment that CPCs offer antiabortion activists is undeniably preferable to making the same claims on the street. CPCs remove the conversation from the volatility of the street, eliminate opposing voices, and ultimately give their employees and volunteers far more control and power over the entire encounter and interaction. The stated desire of CPCs to distance themselves from other antiabortion groups[55] and be the "kind, calm, nonjudgmental" face of the pro-life movement suggests that activists in the movement clearly recognize these advantages.[56] While the movement's sidewalk counselors similarly intend to work in a nonconfrontational manner and be seen as open and helping, the nature and optics of the clinic-front interaction inherently work against this aim and image.

The movement to CPCs and the significant investment in the incremental state politics of abortion are illustrations of how the fight has changed and how the antiabortion movement has learned and developed over time. Proving to be a highly effective tool, the new institutional (versus street-level) fight over abortion that dominates abortion politics is a slow but constantly changing process. As with all of the numbers and specifics of these forms of incremental regulation and their results on the ground in the various states, the results here are subject to fluctuation. This is all the more true as state legislatures increasingly look to add to and modify existing regulations and the resulting laws are challenged in various courts across the judicial system. While the state institutional politics of abortion have been in operation and producing tangible effects for years, they had been underpublicized in comparison to the street politics phase. Simply put, not only are state legislatures receptive forums for antiabortion activists but they are often unnoticed ones, as the national public tends to overlook both state politics and court cases. This changed in the summer of 2013.

The 2013 Texas legislative session was slated to close on May 27, but Gov. Rick Perry called for a 30-day special session that gave him the ability to set the legislative agenda. Antiabortion legislators had entered the regular 2013 legislative session with high hopes, but it had ended with little for them to speak of—close to 20 bills intended to restrict abortion access or further regulate providers failed to be brought to a vote.[57] According to Texas legislative rules, 21 senators are required to vote in favor of bringing bills up for a full vote. While the Republicans enjoyed majorities in both legislative houses, the Senate's 19 Republicans were only able to convince one of their Democratic colleagues to join them in pushing to bring these bills to a vote. The special session stood to give the antiabortion bills a second chance. In addition the special session rules no longer required 21 senators to bring an issue to vote. Rather only a simple majority was needed. Abortion was not originally on the governor's special session agenda, but on June 11, almost halfway through the 30-day special session, Gov. Perry added the issue to the legislative slate. Presented with this opportunity, antiabortion legislators were quick to respond.

Just three days after the addition to the agenda the Texas Senate heard testimony on four bills targeting abortion and abortion clinics. The bills passed committee and made their way to the Senate floor where they were debated into the night of June 18. In a surprising move the bills' sponsor, Sen. Glenn Hegar, cut his proposal to prohibit abortions after the 20th week of pregnancy. The only reason given for his sudden revision was that the 20th-week fetal pain provision was the most controversial, and since the special legislative session ended at midnight on the following Tuesday, the senator wanted to see the bulk of the regulations move forward. The remaining three bills—one requiring clinics to meet ambulatory surgical center standards, another requiring that abortion providers gain admitting privileges at a hospital within 30 miles of the clinics in which they work, and a final one derived from AUL model legislation that increased the cost and waiting time for drug-induced abortions—were subsequently passed by the Senate.[58]

Two days later on Thursday, June 20, the House State Affairs Committee addressed all four abortion bills. In the first attempt to defeat them through a filibuster, the Texas Democratic Party called for abortion-rights advocates to pack the committee meeting and stage a "community filibuster." As the *Austin American-Statesman* reported, "By the time testimony began around 5:45 p.m., more than 250 people had crowded into the State Affairs Committee hearing and an overflow room. By 7:15 p.m., more than 400 people had signed up to testify."[59] As each witness was allotted three minutes to testify, the popular filibuster stood to derail the bills. On Friday the 21st the committee chairman, stating that the public testimony was becoming repetitive, ended the public comments and thus the first attempted filibuster.[60]

In the predawn hours of the following Monday, one day before the proposed end of the special session, the House passed the bills by a vote of 95–34. In doing so the House unlike the Senate had approved the 20th-week fetal pain abortion limitation, requiring that piece of legislation to return to the Senate. The Senate was scheduled to hear the issue on Tuesday with the hope of passing it before the session ended at midnight. While the attempted popular filibuster had helped to publicize the legislative fight to regulate abortion, the conditions were now set to raise the matter to national prominence.

Just after 11:15 a.m. on Tuesday, June 25, Democratic state senator Wendy Davis, wearing running shoes and a dress suit, started her floor address of Texas Senate Bill 5—and did not stop. The Mr. Smith–style filibuster quickly caught national attention. The *Texas Tribune* live-blogged the event, news and social media sites lit up with commentary (President Obama even tweeted about it), and the public began flooding the state capitol. Seeing the time and momentum slipping away, Senate Republicans sought ways of ending the talk-a-thon before the midnight special session deadline.

Her first violation was for straying off topic. The second came around the seven-hour mark when a fellow Democratic senator attempted to help Sen. Davis with a back brace. Shortly after 10 p.m. Lt. Gov. David Dewhurst ruled that Sen. Davis had violated filibuster rules for a third time, and thus her stand was ended by a simple majority vote in the Republican-controlled Senate. The final violation was for again straying off topic when she discussed Texas's preabortion sonogram law that was passed in 2011. The spectators gathered in the viewing gallery vocally rose in opposition when the Republicans voted to end the filibuster, prompting the activity on the floor to descend into chaos and adding a new layer of drama to the events. A portion of the viewing gallery was cleared. Order in the chamber was restored but only temporarily.

The Senate was again engulfed in shouts when the move was made once more to end debate and vote on Senate Bill 5. Democratic senators protested the ruling to end the filibuster and made a string of inquiries about Senate rules in an attempt to fill the remaining time before midnight. Republicans were able to cut off debate and refused to permit numerous Democrats to speak. The crowd in the viewing gallery again contributed to the abortion-rights cause with sustained and vociferous disapproval. This last element—a heckler's filibuster of sorts—proved effective. The din produced made it unclear as to whether the Republicans successfully held a vote on the bill before the midnight deadline.

At the end of the fight the bill was seemingly dead and reproductive-rights advocates and Democrats around Texas and across the country had a new star in Sen. Davis. Her conviction, the physical trial of her one-woman stand, and her personal biography—she was a single mother at age 19, attended community college, and later graduated from Harvard Law School—instantly helped fuel talk of her political future. Of more immediate focus, however, was talk of the Texas abortion bill's future.

Not surprisingly Gov. Perry almost immediately announced a second 30-day special session to start on the coming Monday, July 1.

In doing so the abortion bill was resurrected and the fight resumed with a national audience. Evidence of the issue's increased profile was on full display when five thousand vocal abortion-rights advocates appeared in the Texas capitol to greet the special session and pack the coming hearings and floor debates. In spite of their constant and significant presence at all stages of the political process—both inside and on the streets in front of the capitol—the bill was passed. Gov. Perry signed it into law on July 18, 2013.

The new state law contained the controversial and once-abandoned 20th-week fetal pain cap on abortions as well as provisions mandating that abortion clinics meet surgical center standards and that doctors who perform abortions have admitting privileges at hospitals within 30 miles of the clinic. The law's opponents reminded the viewing public that the law would force roughly 88 percent of the state's clinics to close. As of the summer of 2015 over half of the state's clinics had closed and most are expected to "never reopen, their operators say."[61] This translates to various increased costs for women seeking an abortion in Texas. As *The Upshot* of the *New York Times* reported in terms of travel:

> The average Texas county is now 111 miles from the nearest clinic, up from 72 miles in 2012. This is substantially higher than the national average outside Texas, 59 miles, and more than triple the average in deep red South Carolina, 36 miles. . . .
>
> The impact of House Bill 2 is felt the most in western Texas, which is more rural. Lubbock and Midland each had clinics in 2012. Today, women there have to travel more than 250 miles to get to the nearest clinic: to Fort Worth for women from Lubbock, and to New Mexico for women from Midland.
>
> And these counties aren't alone. A fifth of Texas counties, primarily in the western half of the state, are more than 100 miles farther from a clinic today than they were in 2012.[62]

Moreover the continued operation of seven of the clinics still open at the time of the above accounting was subject to Supreme

Court action in *Whole Woman's Health v. Hellerstedt*—a case challenging House Bill 2. As *The Upshot* noted, while the potential
closure of these clinics would not substantially change the dis-
tances traveled for abortion access in Texas, they stood to have an
effect on the overall cost of abortion.

> For a woman in the average Texas county, the typical cost of an in-state
> abortion would rise 15 percent, to $701. That figure is based on the cost
> of the procedure at eight weeks' gestation (the national average for
> women obtaining abortions) and includes a state-mandated ultra-
> sound and counseling, as well as travel costs. The figure leaves out
> secondary costs, such as lost wages and care for a mother's children,
> which can be significant but are harder to quantify. . . .
>
> These higher prices aren't a coincidence. Converting one of these
> less expensive clinics to an ambulatory surgical center would probably
> cost over $1 million and increase the clinic's annual operating costs by
> $600,000 to $1 million, according to the testimony of Anne Layne-
> Farrar, an economist with expertise in cost-benefit analysis, to the dis-
> trict court as part of the case.[63]

In the broader context of state abortion regulation Texas is now
among the 13 states to ban abortions after 20 weeks.[64] This affirms
its presence in a growing crowd of states looking to aggressively
push the limits of approved regulations on abortion by moving
beyond indirect regulations like mandatory counseling, waiting
period, funding, and TRAP laws, which have been popular. In the
spring of 2013 Arkansas and North Dakota passed the most restrictive abortion laws in the nation by prohibiting abortion on the
basis of fetal heartbeat. Arkansas, citing the time when a heartbeat
can typically be detected when using an abdominal ultrasound,
outlawed abortions at 12 weeks of pregnancy. Alternatively, North
Dakota's prohibition is determined on the case-by-case basis of
heartbeat detectability. Using a transvaginal ultrasound, this
places the limit as early as 6 weeks into a pregnancy. Both North
Dakota's and Arkansas's laws have been struck down by the Eighth

Circuit Court of Appeals as a violation of the Supreme Court's *Casey* limitations on prohibiting abortion before fetal viability outside of the womb. While the Circuit Court struck the laws down, it has also directly encouraged the US Supreme Court to reconsider its ban on previability state regulations of abortion.[65]

At the same time that North Dakota passed its heartbeat ban, the state also prohibited abortions based on fetal genetic abnormalities and instituted a TRAP law requiring doctors providing abortions to have admitting privileges at local hospitals. A few weeks after passing these regulations, North Dakota, like Texas, also banned abortions performed after 20 weeks, citing fetal pain. While some of these states go beyond Texas's House Bill 2, they offer a preview of where the antiabortion movement is headed in pushing the limits of *Casey* in an effort to increasingly limit abortion access. This trend illustrates the importance of *Whole Woman's Health v. Hellerstedt* in understanding the future of abortion politics.

The cumulative and growing effect of this state-level legislative activity is the creation of two separate realities for legal abortion in the United States. In much of the South, the Southwest, and the geographic center of the country stretching from Texas to North Dakota, abortion is becoming a much harder right for women to realize. As of January 2013, before the full course of clinic closures in Texas had run, "roughly 400,000 women of reproductive age (between 15 and 44) live[d] more than 150 miles from the closest clinic in" the center swath of the country.[66] Turning to the targeted regulation of abortion clinics in the South, the *New York Times* reported in May 2014 that

> The Louisiana State Legislature . . . [recently] passed a bill that could force three of the state's five abortion clinics to close, echoing rules passed in Alabama, Mississippi and Texas and raising the possibility of drastically reduced access to abortion across a broad stretch of the South. . . . If the laws in Alabama, Louisiana and Mississippi were to take effect as sponsors envision, and closings play out as clinics have

warned, a woman in New Orleans would be nearly 300 miles from the nearest abortion clinic.[67]

By contrast women in states in the Northeast and West have much greater access to abortion in terms of less regulation and greater clinic availability.

Although the push for increased regulation of abortion is largely geographically bounded, the *McCullen* ruling, much like the rise of crisis pregnancy centers, creates the possibility that the antiabortion movement can still affect—and increase costs for—clinics within states that have historically allowed for greater access to the procedure. *McCullen* may not have erased all clinic-front regulations, but it has invited further litigation to attempt to do so. In the case of Justice Scalia's concurrence, this invitation is quite explicit.[68] The effort to fully undo the complete array of regulatory means will be lengthy and far from certain or unencumbered. Following the cycle of conflict that has defined abortion politics since the late 1970s, antiabortion forces may try to act within, and push, the new parameters set by the Court, but they will be met by abortion-rights advocates who will simultaneously move to defend the existing regulations and work to find new means for replacing those that were defeated.

The controlling opinion in *McCullen*, for example, affirms the virtues of the FACE Act, New York City's antiharassment ordinance, and the use of injunctions to regulate aggressive antiabortion activism. Though less explicit, the opinion also seems to suggest that as conflicts intensify, the state's ability to regulate increases. Clinics then should not likely fully lose the ability to regulate what happens in front of their doors. This maintenance of control, however, is taxing for clinics. Under *McCullen*'s suggested regulation-by-injunction regime, select clinics around the country—such as the Boston clinic that the Court majority admitted had access problems at least one day a week—face increasing isolation, uncertainty, and various costs they have not had to bear since the 1980s and 1990s.

This possible future might be considered in greater detail. Injunctions operate similarly to restraining orders in that individuals and entities ask courts for them on a case-by-case basis. When won, the injunction governs the relationship between the immediately affected parties. In order to seek an injunction a clinic must first sustain some form of illegal activity or harassment, or have strong evidence of its imminent occurrence. Until a clinic secures an injunction—an often lengthy and contested process with an end that is by no means certain—staff and patients must endure what they experience as the various harms of the conflict. What's more, because the United States has a decentralized judicial system, variation is bound to occur in how individual judges interpret individual abortion clinic conflicts, the First Amendment, and the Court's ruling in *McCullen*. The path suggested by *McCullen* will thus produce an inconsistent, localized patchwork of rules controlling what happens in front of individual clinics, thereby significantly increasing uncertainty for clinics.

Governing by injunction also comes with increased direct financial costs for clinics. Abortion providers have to pay lawyers to file and argue for injunctions, and the history of the abortion conflict shows that they must continue to pay lawyers to defend and enforce injunction claims that have been secured. These financial costs are largely transferred to the state when there is a law that regulates clinic-front activism, but in states where injunctions rule, the afflicted party bears the bulk of these costs. This can become a significant burden for clinics, adding to operating expenses in unpredictable ways, especially if and when antiabortion activists challenge awarded injunctions in appellate courts. In this way *McCullen* provides a means for the antiabortion movement to exert significant pressure on clinics and the people they serve.

On a more global level the *McCullen* case and decision increase uncertainty and unnerve abortion-rights advocates because of what they say about the new states of abortion politics. For antiabortion advocates *McCullen* is a clear sign of the progress made by the professionalized antiabortion movement. It shows such observers that the movement's legal instruments are well organized and possess the resources to go on the offensive, which in turn helps them attract more funding and support. More importantly, while they may lose in the lower courts as they did in *McCullen*, the case shows that they have the will and ability to eventually win in the Supreme Court. Finally it shows that the antiabortion movement's institutional abilities, combined with what has been a relatively receptive Supreme Court, create a power that extends beyond friendly states in the South, Southwest, and central plains. With the Court agreeing to hear *Whole Woman's Health v. Hellerstedt*, these fears continue to move from the abstract to the concrete, yet the effects of *Whole Woman's Health* will be the strongest in the states that are most aggressively pursuing access restrictions.

Faced with states like Texas that became more willing to push the limits of the existing incremental politics of abortion, the US Supreme Court had previously refused to hear any of the cases challenging such laws, allowing the lower federal courts to strike down the most aggressive examples using the parameters established under *Casey*. In taking *Whole Woman's Health*, two possibilities were initially created for the Supreme Court to influence the future direction of abortion politics. The case's significance and potential were, however, later complicated by Justice Scalia's sudden passing two and a half weeks before the Court heard oral arguments.

One option for how the Supreme Court could influence the future of abortion politics in *Whole Woman's Health* was that it would reaffirm the dominant understanding of the parameters set in *Casey*, limiting the ability of states to gradually though functionally constrict abortion access and thus allowing threatened clinics to remain open. The other option was that the Supreme Court would affirm some or all of Texas's regulations, thereby setting new limits that antiabortion activists and legislators could work within and then begin to push. While neither route stood to fundamentally change the way abortion politics have operated for decades, the first option—and the only one not potentially altered by Scalia's death—would likely just slow the incremental process and push the antiabortion movement to experiment with new approaches. The second option, on the other hand, would embolden abortion opponents and greatly increase their means to close clinics and erode abortion access in ever-larger swaths of the country. Justice Scalia's passing has complicated this second potential outcome just as it has added new layers of significance to the case and to the future of abortion politics.

Before Justice Scalia died, popular opinion was that antiabortion advocates were well positioned to have the Supreme Court approve of their incremental and indirect approach to regulating abortion. The common understanding was that the four conservatives, joined by the "swing Justice" Kennedy, would let all or part of Texas's law stand, encouraging the antiabortion movement to continue making abortion increasingly inaccessible. Without Scalia popular opinion projected a 4–4 tie. Such a decision would not give the antiabortion movement the national ruling it hoped for from *Whole Woman's Health*, but it would allow the Texas law to stand, and by extension would permit such regulations in Texas, Louisiana, and Mississippi—the three states under the jurisdiction of the Fifth Circuit, which originally affirmed the Texas regulations. Although this outcome would allow the antiabortion movement to pursue its effective incremental strategy of limiting abortion in the immediate region, a follow-up case would be needed to allow the strategy to be clearly permitted across the country as a whole. It is here that one can begin to see how Scalia's death adds new meaning to both the case and the future of abortion politics.

Splitting four to four in *Whole Woman's Health* would strongly encourage if not practically require the Supreme Court to hear a

related case in the not-too-distant future so that it could settle the
law for the whole country. This would drag the Court deeper into
the politics of abortion, something many of its members have
seemingly striven to avoid or at least limit. As a possible sign of
the next contentious abortion case, the Supreme Court temporarily blocked Louisiana's new and closely related abortion regulations just two days after it heard oral arguments in *Whole Woman's
Health*.

Of greatest importance though is that the Texas case starkly
highlights the significance of filling Justice Scalia's vacant Supreme
Court seat in establishing future political opportunities for each
side of the abortion conflict. The near future and continued ad-
vancement of the antiabortion movement's incremental strategy
ultimately depend on a receptive Supreme Court. If Scalia's seat
were filled by a reliably consistent vote in favor of abortion access,
the antiabortion movement would not cease but it would face a
far more difficult immediate future, one where it would continue
to experiment, innovate, and, tellingly, wait for future changes in
its favor on the Supreme Court. The movement has dealt with
Supreme Court constraints before and it can certainly do so again,
but such a shift in the Court would be a severe blow to its efforts.
It would also make the ten years following Justice Alito's replacement of Justice O'Connor seem short lived, and remind observers
of the pace and risks associated with pursuing change through or
contingent on the courts.

Interest in the effects of the Supreme Court's future composition return us to *McCullen's* lessons, which best illustrate the most
significant recent changes within the antiabortion movement that
will affect its ability to continue fighting in the future. Law and
politics scholars have shown that it is possible for well-developed,
savvy legal movements to produce substantive changes even in the
absence of a wholly sympathetic Supreme Court.[69] The preceding
discussion has shown how the antiabortion movement has been
learning, gaining somewhat more favorable political conditions,

and increasing its strength and legal resources for decades; yet there are at least two reasons beyond the loss of Justice Scalia to question the likelihood of its meeting its ultimate stated goal of reversing *Roe* and recriminalizing abortion nationally. The first rests in the stability and ambivalence of public opinion, and the second in the possibility that recent gains by the antiabortion movement will reinvigorate its opponents.

Reliable polling data show that the American public is deeply ambivalent about abortion. As the Pew Research Center on Religion and Public Life notes, "Slightly more than half of the U.S. public (54%) thinks abortion should be legal in all or most cases, a level that has held fairly stable since the mid-1990s (hovering around 50% on the low end, and reaching no higher than 60%) . . . [while] [f]our-in-ten Americans say abortion should be illegal in all or most cases, a level that also has been fairly stable since the mid-1990s."[70] This appears to show a set divide, but when these data are disaggregated one can see that the majority of Americans hold a middle position on abortion. "More than half [56%] say that abortion either should be legal in *most* cases (32%) or should be illegal in *most* cases (24%)."[71] While the latter 24 percent are generally opposed to abortion, only 15 percent of the population believes that abortion should be illegal in *all* cases.[72] The Pew Center is not alone in these findings either. Gallup's data reinforce the above numbers over time and find that in 2015, 29 percent of the population felt that abortion should be legal under any circumstances, an additional 51 percent felt that it should be legal under certain circumstances, and only 19 percent felt that abortion should be illegal under all circumstances.[73]

Beyond the major polling centers a 2015 poll conducted by *Vox* and PerryUndem attempted to dig into the above-cited ambivalence. This poll not only reiterated the more established finding that how one words a polling question matters greatly in how subjects respond, but that "there is a nuance [to beliefs about abortion] that the public conversation typically misses: a factoring in of personal circumstances and beliefs that manifest themselves in deeply held individual views. We've framed our abortion debate all wrong. It isn't black and white—it's thousands of different shades of gray that exist somewhere in the middle."[74] Of note here the poll found that while "more than three-quarters [of those polled] . . . said they held their views on abortion strongly," many did not subscribe to the binary framing of being pro-life or pro-choice. Rather "18 percent of Americans . . . pick 'both' when you ask them to choose between pro-life and pro-choice. Another 21 percent choose neither. Taken together, about four in 10 Americans are eschewing the labels that we typically see as defining the abortion policy debate."[75] In addition, while a significant percentage of those polled do not identify as being clearly pro-choice, they overwhelmingly seem to reject many of the means and effects of the antiabortion movement. When asked, "most Americans (70 percent) think women shouldn't have to travel more than 60 miles to obtain an abortion." Additionally, more than 60 percent also felt that abortion should be affordable and accessible "without added burdens."[76]

The combined message of all this is popular ambivalence over strident loggerheads. The "thousands of different shades of gray that exist somewhere in the middle" have the political potential to create significant limitations for the antiabortion movement. Support for this is borne out by the antiabortion movement's failures to forward more stringent direct and indirect limitations on abortion via the ballot box, and in a history of elections that follow the periodically raised profile of abortion politics. For example, this is seen in the electoral backlashes during the height of the street politics phase when "pro-choice Democrats used the abortion issue to defeat pro-life Republicans in several gubernatorial contests . . . [and] in the 1992 Presidential elections, [when] Bill Clinton received a significant boost from voters who feared the Supreme Court's overruling of *Roe*."[77] It is again seen in the electoral rejections of South Dakota's 2006 and 2008 abortion bans, the 2008

Colorado rejection of a state constitutional amendment granting rights to fertilized eggs, and the 2011 Mississippi rejection of a state bill granting personhood status to fertilized eggs. This history could give pause to the antiabortion movement as the GOP has turned filling Scalia's vacant seat into a presidential-election-year issue, and that broader fight can be used to raise the importance of abortion politics in the 2016 elections.

Along with illustrating the real constraint of public ambivalence, this history argues for the significance of the incremental nature of the antiabortion movement's policy gains and their historically low profile in the press. The converse suggestion is that when the public is aware and mobilized, it can be used to check the antiabortion movement. This serves as a reminder that the history of abortion politics is the history of a movement–countermovement relationship. That is, the opposing sides are locked together in a struggle that cycles in a perpetual spiral. Both sides have significant resources and support in the political establishment as well as in the general public. This has meant that whenever one side moves, the opposing side finds a means to counter and stay in the struggle.

Just as *McCullen* and *Whole Woman's Health* display the antiabortion movement's resources, determination, ability, power, and gains—and thus bolster its confidence—they also work to unnerve and thus spur the opposition. Those in support of abortion access have been in an awkward position since *Roe*. Reproductive-rights advocates won the legal right to abortion before their primary opponents had even formed. As a result they have been in a relative position of weakness ever since. It is always harder to mobilize people to defend something that is already legally protected than it is to organize people to challenge something framed as an injustice. Furthermore since abortion-rights advocates must protect what they have already won, they are constantly reactive and on the defensive. Antiabortion activists, by being positioned as the challengers, are able to determine what form the conflict will take. It is then up to the abortion-rights advocates to find means of responding. This again places antiabortion activists in a relative position of power. Success by one's opponents, however, can shift the calculus.

The risks to the antiabortion movement posed by success and the newly accompanying public attention are clearly seen with the Texas filibusters against Senate Bill 5. Although antiabortion legislators were able to eventually enact new restrictions, it took them two special sessions employing unique legislative rules to do so. This shows that even in a state like Texas that has a history of regulating abortion—lest one forget that *Roe v. Wade* originated as a challenge to Texas's abortion ban—there are legislators willing to resist. When Democratic legislative members called for help from the public, the public showed up in droves. When the matter rose to national attention by way of Sen. Davis's filibuster, "I stand with Wendy" became a rallying cry; abortion-rights advocates were mobilized across the country; and the general public took notice of what had been happening in states across the country. That it is now noted in the national news when states push for regulations similar to those passed by Texas is evidence of the new levels of attention given to abortion politics after the 2013 filibuster.

For now it remains to be seen if reproductive-rights advocates can convert the antiabortion movement's momentum and the fight to fill Scalia's seat into a means for a lasting reinvigoration of abortion rights, one that will have an effect in the states that are pushing the law's limits. In their own friendly states and thus through their own friendly forums these advocates have started to employ new means of taking actions against the antiabortion movement's reach. In November 2015, California enacted the reproductive FACT (Freedom, Accountability, Comprehensive Care, and Transparency) Act, which requires crisis pregnancy centers to inform women seeking their services that "California has public programs that provide immediate free or low-cost access to comprehensive family planning services (including all FDA-approved methods of contraception), prenatal care, and abortion for eligible women. To determine whether you qualify, contact the county social services office at [*telephone number*]." What's more, this information needs to be conveyed in a sign posted "in a conspicuous place where individuals wait that may be easily read by those seeking services from the facility. The notice shall be at least 8.5 inches by 11 inches and written in no less than 22-point type" or distributed via a printed or digital notice at check-in.[78] As one should expect, this law is currently being challenged as a violation of First Amendment rights by a collection of CPCs represented by Alliance Defending Freedom.[79] The results of the court case will contribute one more piece to the evolution of abortion politics. It will determine whether this new reactive tactic of fighting CPCs can spread to other clinic-friendly states.

While the fight unfolds in the states, what either side can do on a national level seems limited in light of Supreme Court rulings, public opinion, and the general history of contemporary abortion politics. Given this, the near future of abortion politics looks to remain much unchanged, with state-based politics in the lead, driving a continued divergence between regions within the country—one side actively moving to regulate abortion out of functional existence, the other preserving its own levels of access, and advocates on each side keeping an eye on how the courts will treat the other side's tactical innovations. Ultimately, as this book has repeatedly shown, the future will continue to be molded by the creativity, resources, and general political conditions that enable or hobble activists working within the parameters set, and reset, by the Court.

ACKNOWLEDGMENTS

I would like to thank a few people whose work was truly indispensable on this project.

First, I would like to thank Kate Wahl, the Publishing Director and Editor in Chief at Stanford University Press and the editor of both of my books with Stanford. While most authors thank their editors near the end of their acknowledgments since editors typically enter the writing process in the later stages, Kate deserves thanks at the outset. She was the one who first raised the idea for this book, encouraged me to write it, found peer reviewers who helped concretely improve the text, and provided valuable feedback at every stage of the process. This book would not exist but for her and her team's help and support.

I also need to thank my father, who has served as my informal editor for decades—on this and so many other writing projects. He has read and given me feedback on every draft and has shown something akin to superhuman levels of patience in never giving any signs of hesitance at being asked to face yet another version.

Finally, I need to thank Elisha, Lila, and Reed. As I said in the dedication, you have each contributed in your own ways to this book, and it certainly would not exist without your help in creating a space within which I could write it.

NOTES

PREFACE

1. Nina Martin, "The Coming Showdown: A Year for Reproductive Rights," *Public Radio International*, January 11, 2016, http://www.pri.org/stories/2016-01-11/coming-showdown-year-reproductive-rights.

2. Vic Vela, "Taxes, Housing and More: Your Guide to the 2016 Legislative Session," *Colorado Public Radio*, January 12, 2016, https:/www.cpr.org/news/story/taxes-housing-and-more-your-guide-2016-legislative-session.

3. I have chosen to refer to the opposing sides of this conflict as "antiabortion" and "abortion rights" as opposed to "Pro-Life" and "Pro-Choice." While my labels are less common and not the chosen titles of the respective groups, they are more directly related to the subject of contention: the legality of abortion.

PART I. VIOLENCE, LAW, AND ABORTION POLITICS

1. John Kifner, "Anti-Abortion Killings: The Arrest; Suspect in Clinic Killings Eludes Hunt but Is Caught in 3d Attack, in Virginia," *New York Times*, January 1, 1995.

2. John Kifner, "Anti-Abortion Killings: The Overview; Gunman Kills 2 at Abortion Clinics in Boston Suburb," *New York Times*, December 31, 1994.

3. Ibid.

4. Fred Contrada, "Shootings at Clinics Shock WMass—Counseling Facilities on Alert as Result of Brookline Slayings," *Union-News (Springfield, MA)*, December 31, 1994.

5. Laurie Goodstein and Pierre Thomas, "Clinic Killings Follow Years of Antiabortion Violence," *Washington Post*, January 17, 1995.

6. "Civil Rights Division Freedom of Access to Reproductive Health Clinics and Places of Religious Worship," accessed September 30, 2013, http://www.justice.gov/crt/about/spl/face.php.

7. "Abortion Clinic Buffer Zone Bill Filed," *Worcester Telegram & Gazette (MA)*, December 30, 1997; "A Bill's Long Road to a Hearing, Rep. Story Fought to Get Hearing for Abortion Clinic Bill," *Daily Hampshire Gazette (Northampton, MA)*, July 6, 1998.

8. "Bill's Long Road to a Hearing."

9. Rep. Story as quoted in "Story Bill to Protect Abortion Clinics Faces Thursday Hearing," *Daily Hampshire Gazette (Northampton, MA)*, April 14, 1999.

10. Doherty as quoted in "Abortion Clinic Buffers Debated," *Worcester Telegram & Gazette (MA)*, April 16, 1999.

11. "Amid Intrigue, Abortion Bill at Center of Heated Battle," *Daily Hampshire Gazette (Northampton, MA)*, June 23, 1999.

12. Ellen Silberman, "Committee Postpones Clinic Buffer Vote," *Boston Herald*, June 22, 1999.

13. Bronislaus B. Kush, "Anti-Abortion Group Protests Bill," *Worcester Telegram & Gazette (MA)*, July 15, 2000.

14. Section 120E 1/2(b)(1-2) of Mass.Gen.L. ch. 266.

15. Karen Crummy, "House OKs Weakened Bill on Clinic Protests," *Boston Herald*, July 29, 2000.

16. Rep. Story as quoted in, "Abortion Buffer Zone Bill Heads to Senate," *Daily Hampshire Gazette (Northampton, MA)*, July 29, 2000.

17. Quoted in Crummy, "House OKs Weakened Bill on Clinic Protests."

18. Susan Greenleaf, "Uses Law Degree to Help the Most Disadvantaged, the Unborn," *Massachusetts News,* July 2001.

19. McGuire v. Reilly, 122 F. Supp. 2d 97 (D. Mass. 2000).

20. J. M. Lawrence, "AG Wants Fed Judge to Clarify Buffer Zone Injunction," *Boston Herald,* November 22, 2000.

21. Reilly as quoted in ibid.

22. "Beginnings," accessed July 24, 2015, http://en.pusc.it/info/speciale-xxv-anniversario/origini.

23. McGuire v. Reilly, 260 F.3d 36 (1st Cir. 2001).

24. McGuire v. Reilly, 230 F. Supp.2d 189 (D. Mass. 2002).

25. McGuire v. Reilly, 285 F. Supp.2d 82 (D. Mass. 2003).

26. McGuire v. Reilly, 386 F.3d 45 (1st Cir. 2004).

27. McGuire v. Reilly, 271 F. Supp.2d 335 (D. Mass. 2003).

28. Christina Wallace, "Bill Would Expand Buffer Zones," *Metro Boston*, December 29, 2005.

29. As quoted in Tony Lee, "Buffer Zone Bill Gets through Senate; Pro-Lifers Upset," *Metro Boston*, October 24, 2007.

30. As quoted in Casey Ross, "Patrick Signs Abortion Buffer Zone Bill," *Boston Herald Blogs*, November 13, 2007.

31. National Abortion Federation, "NAF Violence and Disruption Statistics," n.d., http://www.prochoice.org/pubs_research/publications/downloads/about_abortion/stats_table2010.pdf.

32. Joshua C. Wilson, *The Street Politics of Abortion: Speech, Violence, and America's Culture Wars*, The Cultural Lives of Law (Stanford: Stanford University Press, 2013).

33. Jessica Fargen, "Activists Sue over Ban on Abort Protest in Buffer Zone," *Boston Herald*, January 19, 2008.

34. Patrick Doyle, "Resurrection," *Boston Magazine*, November 2012.

35. ADF, McCullen v. Coakley Complaint (D. Mass. 2008).

36. McCullen v. Coakley, 573 F. Supp.2d 382 (D. Mass. 2008).

37. McCullen v. Coakley, 571 F.3d 167 (1st Cir. 2009).

38. Ibid.

39. McCullen v. Coakley, 759 F. Supp.2d 133 (D. Mass. 2010).

40. McCullen v. Coakley, 844 F. Supp.2d 206 (D. Mass. 2012).

41. McCullen v. Coakley, 708 F.3d 1 (1st Cir. 2013).

42. McCullen v. Coakley, 133 S. Ct. 2857 (2013).

43. Michael DePrimo, by phone, November 1, 2013.

44. McCullen v. Coakley 573 U.S. 3 (2014). Scalia, pp. 1, 3.

45. Ibid., pp. 9–10. Emphasis added.

46. Ibid., pp. 4–5.

47. Ibid., pp. 27–28.

48. Ibid., p. 21.

49. Ibid., p. 23.

50. Ibid., pp. 24–25.

51. Alana Semuels, "Abortion Foes Get up Close and Personal after Court Erases Buffer Zones," *Los Angeles Times*, July 2, 2014.

52. An Act to Promote Public Safety and Protect Access to Reproductive Health Care Facilities, S.2281, 188th (2013–14) (sponsor Harriette Chandler), https://malegislature.gov/Bills/188/Senate/S2281.

53. Steve LeBlanc, "Group Urges Caution on New Mass. Buffer Zone Bill," *WBUR*, July 8, 2014.

PART II. FROM ALLIES TO ALLIANCES IN THE ANTIABORTION MOVEMENT

1. Massachusetts Citizens for Life, "Massachusetts Citizens for Life: Mission, History, Direction," accessed October 28, 2013.

2. Roger M. Smith, "An Almost-Christian Nation? Constitutional Consequences of the Rise of the Religious Right," in *Evangelicals and Democracy in America, Vol. 1: Religion and Society*, ed. Steven Brint and Jean Reith Schroedel (New York: Russell Sage Foundation, 2009), 329–55; Daniel K. Williams, "The GOP's Abortion Strategy: Why Pro-Choice Republicans Became Pro-Life in the 1970s," *Journal of Policy History* 23, no. 4 (2011): 513–39.

3. Massachusetts Citizens for Life, "Massachusetts Citizens for Life: Mission, History, Direction," 7.

4. See, for example, Catherine Albiston, "The Rule of Law and the Litigation Process: The Paradox of Losing by Winning," *Law and Society Review* 33, no. 4 (1999): 869–910; Kristin Bumiller, *The Civil Rights Society: The Social Construction of Victims* (Baltimore: Johns Hopkins University Press, 1992); Mary Ann Glendon, *Rights Talk: The Impoverishment of Political Discourse* (New York: Free Press, 1993); Duncan Kennedy, "The Critique of Rights in Critical Legal Studies," in *Left Liberalism/Left Critique* (Durham, NC: Duke University Press Books, 2002), 178; Stuart A. Scheingold, *The Politics of Rights: Lawyers, Public Policy, and Political Change*, 2nd ed. (Ann Arbor: University of Michigan Press, 2004).

5. The amendments were later undone by the Supreme Judicial Court of Massachusetts, in Mary Moe & others v. Secretary of Administration and Finance & others (1981).

6. Philip Moran, by phone, October 28, 2013.

7. Ibid.

8. Ibid.

9. "Internet Archive Wayback Machine," April 1, 2003, https://web.archive.org/web/20030401000000*/http://plldf.org.

10. "Pro Life Legal, Pro-Life Legal Defense Fund, Inc. Newton, MA Home," accessed February 8, 2016, http://plldf.org/.

11. "Pro Life Legal, Pro-Life Legal Defense Fund, Inc. Newton, MA Blog," accessed July 28, 2015, http://plldf.org/blog.html.

12. "Pro Life Legal, Pro-Life Legal Defense Fund, Inc. Newton, MA Professors' Corner," accessed February 8, 2016, http://plldf.org/newsandevents/professorscorner.html.

13. "Pro Life Legal Defense Fund – Newsletter," accessed February 8, 2016, http://plldf.org/newsandevents/newsletter.html.

14. "Advocacy conglomerate" is a term used by Kevin Den Dulk. See "Purpose-Driven Lawyers: Evangelical Cause Lawyering and the Culture War," in *The Cultural Lives of Cause Lawyers*, ed. Austin Sarat and Stuart Scheingold (New York: Cambridge University Press, 2008), 56–78.

15. Philip Moran, by phone, October 28, 2013.

16. "Frequently Asked Questions – Alliance Defending Freedom," accessed November 1, 2013, http://www.alliancedefendingfreedom.org/about/faq.

17. "About Us > Leadership – Alliance Defending Freedom," accessed February 8, 2016, http://web.archive.org/web/20140325232906/http://www.alliancedefendingfreedom.org/about/leadership#Brooks.

18. Alliance Defending Freedom, "Leadership," accessed February 8, 2016, http://www.adflegal.org/about-us/leadership.

19. "About Us > Leadership – Alliance Defending Freedom," accessed July 28, 2015, http://www.adflegal.org/about-us/leadership.

20. "Frequently Asked Questions – Alliance Defending Freedom," accessed November 1, 2013. http://www.alliancedefendingfreedom.org/about/faq. Emphasis added.

21. See, for example, Daniel Williams, *God's Own Party: The Making of the Christian Right* (New York: Oxford University Press, 2010).

22. Steven Teles, *The Rise of the Conservative Legal Movement: The Battle for Control of the Law* (Princeton: Princeton University Press, 2010), 58.

23. Department of the Treasury, Internal Revenue Service, Form 990, Alliance Defending Freedom, FY 2012 ("Contributions and grants" listed at $38,943,749).

24. Department of the Treasury, Internal Revenue Service, Form 990, American Center for Law and Justice, 2012 ("Return of Organization Exempt from Income Tax," part 2, p. 2).

25. Department of the Treasury, Internal Revenue Service, Form 990, Alliance Defending Freedom, FY 2012 ("Contributions and grants" listed at $38,943,749).

26. Alliance Defending Freedom, "FAQ," accessed November 5, 2013, http://www.adflegal.org/About/FAQ.

27. Ibid.

28. Hans J. Hacker, *The Culture of Conservative Christian Litigation* (Lanham, MD: Rowman & Littlefield, 2005), 188.

29. Alliance Defending Freedom, "Attorneys," accessed July 28, 2015, http://www.adflegal.org/about-us/attorneys.

30. Erik Eckholm, "Legal Alliance Gains Host of Court Victories for Conservative Christian Movement," *New York Times*, May 11, 2014.

31. Alliance Defending Freedom, "FAQ."

32. Teles, *Rise of the Conservative Legal Movement*, 254–55.

33. Alliance Defending Freedom, "FAQ."

34. Ibid.

35. Ibid. Emphasis added.

36. Ibid.

37. See "Rule 6.1: Voluntary Pro Bono Publico Service – The Center for Professional Responsibility," accessed February 8, 2016, http://www.americanbar.org/groups/professional_responsibility/publications/model_rules_of_professional_conduct/rule_6_1_voluntary_pro_bono_publico_service.html.

38. Alliance Defending Freedom, "History," accessed November 7, 2013, http://www.alliancedefendingfreedom.org/about/history.

39. Alliance Defending Freedom, "FAQ." Emphasis added.

40. Ibid. Emphasis in original.

41. Ibid. Emphasis added.

42. Quoted in Erik Eckholm, "Legal Alliance Gains Host of Court Victories for Conservative Christian Movement," *New York Times*, May 11, 2014.

43. Regent University School of Law, "The Regent Law Difference," accessed November 7, 2013, http://www.regent.edu/acad/schlaw/whyregentlaw/whyregentlaw.cfm.

44. Alliance Defense Fund, "Blackstone Legal Fellowship," n.d., http://www.alliancedefensefund.org/Home/ADFContent?cid=3148.

45. "Blackstone – Legal Fellowship – A Ministry of Alliance Defending Freedom," accessed July 29, 2015, http://www.blackstonelegalfellowship.org/About/History.

46. Alliance Defending Freedom, "Young Lawyers Academy," accessed July 29, 2016, http://www.adflegal.org/training/young-lawyers-academy.

47. Ibid.

48. Charles H. Oates, "The Regent University Law Library: The First Thirty Years," *Regent University Law Review* 21 (2008): 229–74.

49. Michael DePrimo, by phone, November 1, 2013.

50. "The Rutherford Institute: About Us," accessed July 27, 2015, https://www.rutherford.org/about.

51. "A First: Federal-State Lawsuit against Abortion Protesters," *New York Times*, accessed November 4, 2013, http://www.nytimes.com/1995/06/22/nyregion/a-first-federal-state-lawsuit-against-abortion-protesters.html.

52. American Family Association, "About Us," accessed July 27, 2015, http://www.afa.net/who-is-afa/about-us/.

53. Hacker, *Culture of Conservative Christian Litigation*, 92.

54. Ibid., 92.

55. Michael DePrimo, by phone, November 1, 2013.

56. Ibid.

57. Alliance Defense Fund, "ADF Launches Legal Effort to Protect Churches from Government Intrusion," accessed April 14, 2010, http://www.adfmedia.org/News/PRDetail/3972.

58. Alliance Defending Freedom, "Kevin Theriot," accessed July 31, 2015, http://www.adflegal.org/detailspages/biography-details/kevin-theriot.

PART III. THE PAST AS THE POSSIBLE FUTURE OF ABORTION POLITICS

1. Daniel K. Williams, "The GOP's Abortion Strategy: Why Pro-Choice Republicans Became Pro-Life in the 1970s," *Journal of Policy History* 23, no. 4 (2011): 513–39.

2. See chs. 2 and 3 in Kristin Luker, *Abortion and the Politics of Motherhood* (Berkeley: University of California Press, 1985).

3. Ibid., chs. 3–5.

4. New York, Washington, Alaska, and Hawaii were four states that repealed their abortion laws. California, Oregon, New Mex-

ico, Colorado, Kansas, Arkansas, and every state along the Atlantic coast from Florida up to Delaware reformed their abortion laws.

5. Williams, "The GOP's Abortion Strategy."

6. Ibid.

7. Ibid.

8. Ibid., 513.

9. See ch. 2 in Clyde Wilcox and Carin Robinson, *Onward Christian Soldiers? The Religious Right in American Politics*, 4th rev. ed. (Boulder, CO: Westview Press, 2010).

10. Engel v. Vitale, 370 U.S. 421 (1962); Abington School Dist. v. Schempp, 374 U.S. 203 (1963).

11. Paul S. Boyer, "The Evangelical Resurgence in 1970s American Protestantism," in *Rightward Bound: Making America Conservative in the 1970s*, ed. Bruce J. Schulman and Julian E. Zelizer (Cambridge, MA: Harvard University Press, 2008), 36.

12. Wilcox and Robinson, *Onward Christian Soldiers?* 11.

13. Williams, "The GOP's Abortion Strategy"; Daniel Williams, *God's Own Party: The Making of the Christian Right* (New York: Oxford University Press, 2010).

14. Falwell as quoted in Matthew D. Lassiter, "Inventing Family Values," in Schulman and Zelizer, *Rightward Bound*, 26.

15. Lassiter, "Inventing Family Values."

16. James Risen and Judy Thomas, *Wrath of Angels: The American Abortion War* (New York: Basic Books, 1998), 127.

17. Wilcox and Robinson, *Onward Christian Soldiers?* 43.

18. Ronald Reagan as quoted in "God in America – Transcripts: Hour Six – 'Of God and Caesar,'" *God in America*, accessed January 8, 2015, http://www.pbs.org/godinamerica/transcripts/hour-six .html.

19. Williams, *God's Own Party*, 8.

20. Deana A. Rohlinger, *Abortion Politics, Mass Media, and Social Movements in America* (New York: Cambridge University Press, 2014), 52–77.

21. Guttmacher Institute, "State Policies in Brief: Requirements for Ultrasound," June 1, 2014, http://www.guttmacher.org/state-center/spibs/spib_RFU.pdf. Cases heard by the Court include Frisby v. Schultz, 108 S. Ct. 2495 (1988); Bray v. Alexandria Women's Health Clinic, 506 U.S. 263 (1993); National Organization for Women, Inc. v. Scheidler, 510 U.S. 249 (1994); Madsen v. Women's Health Center, Inc., 512 U.S. 753 (1994); Schenck v. Pro-Choice Network of Western NY, 519 U.S. 357 (1997); Hill v. Colorado, 530 U.S. 703 (2000); Scheidler v. National Organization for Women, Inc., 537 U.S. 393 (2003); Scheidler v. National Organization for Women, Inc., 547 U.S. 9 (2006); McCullen v. Coakley 573 U.S. (2014). Cases that the Court has not heard but that individual members responded to with written opinions in relation to denials of cert. include Scalia, Winfield et al. v. Kaplan et al., U.S. (1994); and Lawson v. Murray, 515 U.S. 94–1450, 1110 (1995); Williams v. Planned Parenthood Shasta-Diablo, Inc., 520 U.S. 1133 (1997); Lawson v. Murray, 525 U.S. 955 (1998); Scalia, Cloer v. Gynecology Clinic, Inc. (Scalia, J., dissenting), 528 U.S. 1099 (2000).

22. The Guttmacher Institute is a good source for a detailed cataloguing of the antiabortion movement's state regulatory successes.

23. Thornburgh v. American College of Obstetricians & Gynecologists, 476 U.S. 747, 759 (1986).

24. "Thornburgh-v-ACOG-1985-box20-memoFriedtoAlito-June3.pdf," accessed February 8, 2016, https://www.archives.gov/news/samuel-alito/accession-060-89-216/Thornburgh-v-ACOG-1985-box20-memoFriedtoAlito-June3.pdf.

25. Ibid., 9. Emphasis in original.

26. Ibid., 16.

27. Ibid., 15.

28. Ibid., 17.

29. Ibid.

30. Webster v. Reproductive Health Services, 492 U.S. 490 (1989).

31. Marshall Medoff, "The Determinants and Impact of State Abortion Restrictions," *American Journal of Economics and Sociology* 61, no. 2 (2002): 482.

32. Planned Parenthood of Southeastern Pa. v. Casey, 505 U.S. 833 (1992).

33. Ibid.

34. Ibid. Emphasis added.

35. "Does a Fetus Feel Pain at 20 Weeks?" accessed November 18, 2015, http://www.factcheck.org/2015/05/does-a-fetus-feel-pain -at-20-weeks/.

36. *Frontline*, "State Regulation of Abortion," n.d., http:// www.pbs.org/wgbh/pages/frontline/clinic/etc/map.html.

37. *Frontline*, "The Last Abortion Clinic," November 8, 2005, http://www.pbs.org/wgbh/pages/frontline/clinic/interviews/sam- uelson.html.

38. Americans United for Life, "History," accessed July 17, 2014, http://www.aul.org/about-aul/history/.

39. Americans United for Life, "Order Model Legislation," accessed August 19, 2015, http://www.aul.org/legislative-resources/ order-model-legislation/.

40. *RealClear Politics*, "The Other GOP Wave: State Legislatures," accessed October 30, 2015, http://www.realclearpolitics.com/arti- cles/2014/11/11/the_other_gop_wave_state_legislatures__124626.html.

41. Heather D. Boonstra and Elizabeth Nash, "A Surge of State Abortion Restrictions Puts Providers—and the Women They Serve— in the Crosshairs," *Guttmacher Policy Review* 17, no. 1 (Winter 2014), http://www.guttmacher.org/pubs/gpr/17/1/gpr170109.html.

42. Guttmacher Institute, "State Laws on Ultrasound Abor- tion - spib_RFU.pdf," accessed August 20, 2015, http://www.gutt- macher.org/statecenter/spibs/spib_RFU.pdf.

43. Guttmacher Institute, "State Abortion Laws - spib_OAL. pdf," accessed August 20, 2015, http://www.guttmacher.org/state- center/spibs/spib_OAL.pdf.

44. Guttmacher Institute, "Abortion, Health Insurance, State Laws - spib_RICA.pdf," accessed August 20, 2015, http://www. guttmacher.org/statecenter/spibs/spib_RICA.pdf.

45. Guttmacher Institute, "State Abortion Laws - spib_OAL .pdf."

46. Kim Soffen, "How Texas Could Set National Template for Limiting Abortion Access," *New York Times*, August 19, 2015, http://www.nytimes.com/2015/08/20/upshot/how-texas-could-set-national-template-for-limiting-abortion-access.html.

47. Guttmacher Institute, "Targeted Regulation of Abortion Providers, Abortion Clinic Regulation - spib_TRAP.pdf," accessed August 19, 2015, http://www.guttmacher.org/statecenter/spibs/spib_TRAP.pdf.

48. Kate Pickert, "What Choice?" *Time*, January 14, 2013, http://content.time.com/time/magazine/article/0,9171,2132761,00.html.

49. Guttmacher Institute, "'Choose Life' License Plates - spib_CLLP.pdf," accessed November 10, 2015, http://www.guttmacher.org/statecenter/spibs/spib_CLLP.pdf.

50. "Guttmacher Institute State Update: Pending Legislation," accessed November 10, 2015, http://www.guttmacher.org/statecenter/updates/.

51. Pam Belluck, "Pregnancy Centers Gain Influence in Anti-Abortion Fight," *New York Times*, January 4, 2013, sec. Health, http://www.nytimes.com/2013/01/05/health/pregnancy-centers-gain-influence-in-anti-abortion-fight.html.

52. Ibid.

53. Ibid.

54. Ibid.

55. Ibid.

56. Nancy Gibbs, "The Grass-Roots Abortion War," *Time*, February 15, 2007, http://content.time.com/time/magazine/article/0,9171,1590444,00.html.

57. Chuck Lindell, "Perry Adds Abortion to Session – Proposed Regulations That Failed in Regular Session Need Fewer Votes to Pass Now," *Austin American-Statesman (TX)*, June 12, 2013.

58. Chuck Lindell, "Abortion Debate Extends into Night – GOP Senators Argue for Safety While Democrats Vow to Resist Passage," *Austin American-Statesman (TX)*, June 19, 2013.

59. Mike Ward, Chuck Lindell, and Tim Eaton, "House Takes on Abortion, Districts – Chamber Also Gets to Other Hot-Button

Issues, Including Road Funding," *Austin American-Statesman (TX)*, June 21, 2013.

60. Associated Press, "Texas: Abortion Curbs Advance," *New York Times*, June 22, 2013, late ed. – final ed., sec. National Briefing: Southwest.

61. Sophie Novack, "Texas Is Permanently Shutting Abortion Clinics and the Supreme Court Can't Do Anything about It," *National Journal*, May 5, 2014, http://www.nationaljournal.com/health-care/texas-is-permanently-shutting-abortion-clinics-and-the-supreme-court-can-t-do-anything-about-it-20140505.

62. Soffen, "How Texas Could Set National Template for Limiting Abortion Access."

63. Ibid.

64. Guttmacher Institute, "State Abortion Laws - spib_OAL.pdf"; "Scott Walker Signs Abortion Ban Bill," *US News and World Report*, accessed August 20, 2015, http://www.usnews.com/news/politics/articles/2015/07/20/gop-presidential-hopeful-walker-signs-abortion-ban-bill.

65. *SCOTUSblog*, "Appeals Court Wants Court to Take New Look at Abortion," accessed August 20, 2015, http://www.scotusblog.com/2015/07/appeals-court-wants-court-to-take-new-look-at-abortion/.

66. Michael Keller and Allison Yarrow, "The Geography of Abortion Access," *Daily Beast*, January 22, 2013, http://www.thedailybeast.com/articles/2013/01/22/the-geography-of-abortion-access.html.

67. Jeremy Alford and Erik Eckholm, "With New Bill, Abortion Limits Spread in South," *New York Times*, May 21, 2014, http://www.nytimes.com/2014/05/22/us/politics/new-bill-spreads-abortion-limits-in-south.html.

68. McCullen v. Coakley, 573 U.S. (2014). Scalia, pp. 9–10.

69. See Charles R. Epp, *The Rights Revolution: Lawyers, Activists, and Supreme Courts in Comparative Perspective* (Chicago: University of Chicago Press, 1998); and Steven Teles, *The Rise of the*

Conservative Legal Movement: The Battle for Control of the Law (Princeton: Princeton University Press, 2010).

70. 1615 L. Street et al., "Public Opinion on Abortion Slideshow," Pew Research Center's Religion and Public Life Project, accessed November 19, 2015, http://www.pewforum.org/2013/01/16/public-opinion-on-abortion-slideshow/.

71. Ibid. Emphasis in original.

72. Ibid.

73. Gallup.com, "Abortion," accessed November 23, 2015, http://www.gallup.com/poll/1576/Abortion.aspx.

74. Sarah Kliff, "What Americans Actually Think of Abortion," *Vox*, accessed November 23, 2015, http://www.vox.com/a/abortion-decision-statistics-opinions.

75. Ibid.

76. Ibid.

77. Neal Devins, "How Planned Parenthood v. Casey (Pretty Much) Settled the Abortion Wars," *Yale Law Journal* 118 (2009): 1318–54, 1327, accessed January 1, 2009, http://scholarship.law.wm.edu/facpubs/343.

78. "Bill Text - AB-775 Reproductive FACT Act," accessed November 19, 2015, https://leginfo.legislature.ca.gov/faces/billNavClient.xhtml?bill_id=201520160AB775.

79. Alliance Defending Freedom, "Calif. Law Forces pro-Life Centers to Promote Abortion, ADF Files Suit," accessed November 19, 2015, http://www.adfmedia.org/News/PRDetail/9776.